Leaven for the Modern World:

Catholic Social Teaching and Catholic Education

Ronald Krietemeyer

National Catholic Educational Association

© 2000
National Catholic Educational Association
1077 30th Street, NW, Suite 100
Washington, DC 20007-3852

ISBN 1-55833-246-4

Table of Contents

Foreword

"This is my commandment, that you love one another as I have loved you. No one has greater love than this, to lay down one's life for one's friends...And I appointed you to go and bear fruit, fruit that will last, so that the Father will give you whatever you ask him in my name."

— John 15: 12-13, 16

In *Leaven for the Modern World: Catholic Social Teaching and Catholic Education*, Ronald Krietemeyer states that the Church's social teaching "is at the heart of the Church's mission and, therefore, at the heart of Catholic education. It is a tradition that offers a unique and challenging vision of how to live a dignified life, a life of commitment to the common good, a life dedicated to God's great commandment of love."

This brief statement clearly explains Catholic social teaching and its implications in the world. All people are children of God, created in God's image and likeness. Everyone deserves to be treated with dignity and is therefore entitled to the basic human necessities of life. Unfortunately, since this does not always occur in daily life, the Church calls everyone to work for social justice.

Mr. Krietemeyer stresses the importance of teaching children and students in Catholic education about Catholic social teaching and its implementation and abuse in daily life. He notes that "If educators are expected to bring the values of Catholic social teaching into every dimension of their work, then they need the opportunity to deepen their understanding of this teaching. If undertaken successfully, such efforts will enrich Catholic educators personally, will improve their teaching, and will enhance the Catholic identity of their schools."

Since many Catholic educators need to deepen their own understanding of this teaching, the first part of the book addresses the actual teaching itself and its biblical foundations. The second part of the book identifies the elements and steps that are necessary for the successful integration of Catholic social teaching, describes the personal and social traits found in Catholic school graduates who have learned and assimilated these values, and provides examples of how teachers in various disciplines can incorporate this teaching into their classes. "Samples and Examples" is particularly useful because it provides concrete examples of how Catholic social teaching can be incorporated not only in classes such as social studies, math, and religion but also into faculty development. The appendices provide a comprehensive list of sources—both Church documents and other resources—for those who seek to learn more about Catholic social teaching.

Leaven for the Modern World: Catholic Social Teaching and Catholic Education is an excellent resource for Catholic educators. I strongly urge administrators, teachers, campus ministers, and board members to view this book as an ideal tool in their efforts to improve their awareness for Catholic social teaching and to incorporate that teaching in the lives of their students.

Brian Vaccaro
Co-editor
NCEA Secondary Schools Department

Introduction

I magine a Catholic high school where students are involved in a service project, volunteering at a local shelter for the homeless. At the same time, these students are studying what the Church teaches about social justice. They learn that works of charity are not a substitute for basic justice. They look deeper into the causes of homelessness, and they learn about the critical need for more affordable housing. Knowing that housing is a basic moral right in Catholic teaching, they go to a city council hearing and testify on behalf of a proposal that will bring more affordable housing to their community. They talk about the common good and argue that the whole community will be better off if the elected officials vote to approve the proposal.

Such public witness by these students is one indication of how their Catholic education has made a difference. It has helped them to become value-based leaders and agents for human dignity and justice in the community. It has helped them to become truly Catholic.

In an effort to clarify and deepen their Catholic identity, many Catholic schools have begun to give increased attention to the social teaching of the Church. This teaching encompasses a rich set of values and teaching documents that give guidance to people of faith regarding how to think and act in the world. Understanding these documents and promoting these values is an important element of any school's effort to strengthen its Catholic identity.

Unfortunately, the contemporary American Catholic Church has not done a satisfactory job of educating its members about the Church's social teaching. As the U.S. bishops frankly admit in a recent statement, "Many Catholics do not adequately understand that the social teaching of the Church is an essential part of the Catholic faith. This poses a serious challenge for all Catholics, since it weakens our capacity to be a Church that is true to the demands of the Gospel."[1]

It should not be surprising, therefore, that many educators and students in Catholic schools are not well versed in the Church's social teaching. They are not very familiar with the theology that underlies this teaching, and they have not been exposed to the content of the documents that comprise the teaching. If educators are expected to bring the values of Catholic social teaching into every dimension of their work, then they need the opportunity to deepen their understanding of this teaching. If undertaken successfully, such efforts will enrich Catholic educators personally, will improve their teaching, and will enhance the Catholic identity of their schools.

The challenge before teachers and administrators is to ensure that Catholic social teaching is integrated into the mainstream of Catholic educational institutions and programs. Toward that end, the material in this book presents a set of ideas and resources that can be used to incorporate Catholic social teaching more fully into Catholic secondary education. Part One of the book consists of three chapters that focus on the foundations and content of Catholic social teaching. Chapter 1 provides a rationale for treating the Church's social teaching as a necessary and integral part of Catholic identity. Chapters 2 and 3 offer a discussion of the biblical roots of Catholic social teaching and a summary of the major themes of the Church's social teaching documents from the last 100 years. These are especially important chapters for educators who are not familiar with the basic content of Catholic social teaching and would like a brief overview of the key principles and values from that teaching.

Part Two of the book provides a set of resources to help teachers and administrators integrate Catholic social teaching into their schools. Chapter 4 suggests a list of key elements that might be part of a comprehensive strategy for infusing Catholic social values into the life of a Catholic school. Chapter 5 suggests a sample planning process as a guide for carrying out the practical steps necessary to effectively implement the goals discussed here. In Chapter 6, the reader will find a set of reflections on the virtues and skills that one might expect to see in Catholic school graduates who have learned and assimilated the core values of Catholic social teaching. Chapter 7 describes a series of concrete examples demonstrating what some schools have done to infuse Catholic social teaching into different dimension of academic and student life.

Finally, the appendices contain an annotated list of readings and resources that teachers can use to further deepen their understanding of Catholic social teaching and a chronological listing of official Church documents on social teaching. Readers are encouraged to use and adapt the material in this book so that it fits their own circumstances as individual teachers or as decision-makers in Catholic schools.

In exploring the material in this book, it will be useful to keep in mind the message articulated by the U.S. bishops in 1998:

> *Just as the social teaching of the Church is integral to the Catholic faith, the social justice dimensions of teaching are integral to Catholic education and catechesis. They are an essential part of Catholic identity and formation.*
>
> *The values of the Church's social teaching must not be treated as tangential or optional. They must be a core part of teaching and formation. Without our social teaching, schools, catechetical programs, and other formation programs would be offering an incomplete presentation of our Catholic tradition. This would fall short of our mission and would be a serious loss for those in our educational and catechetical programs.[2]*

These words from the U.S. bishops present both a profound challenge and a rich opportunity for educators in Catholic schools. This book is a tool to help educators meet that challenge and take advantage of that opportunity.

Part I

Foundations
of Catholic Social Teaching

Chapter 1

Catholic Social Teaching:
A Key to Catholic Identity

Our faith is profoundly social. We cannot be called truly
"Catholic" unless we hear and heed the Church's call to
serve those in need and work for justice and peace. We
cannot call ourselves followers of Jesus unless we take up
his mission of bringing "good news to the poor, liberty to
captives, and new sight to the blind" (cf. Lk. 4:18).

— National Conference of Catholic Bishops[3]

In considering the role of Catholic social teaching in Catholic education, it is useful to begin by addressing the "why" questions. Why is Catholic social teaching a key part of Catholic identity? Why is the Church's social mission integral to the very definition of the Church? Why is commitment to social justice an essential part of the Catholic faith?

More specifically, Catholic educators might ask, why should we focus on this part of the Church's tradition? Given the challenging nature of the Church's social teaching and the complexity of implementing it in the contemporary world, why bother? Why should those of us who work in Catholic schools worry about applying Catholic moral values in the social arena? Why not leave the function of promoting social justice to the activists and the specialists?

One answer to these questions can be stated quite briefly — because to teach in a Catholic school is to be part of a wider Church whose meaning, mandate, and mission have justice as an essential component.

> An integral part of Catholic identity is the Church's social teaching. This teaching is at the heart of the Church's mission and, therefore, at the heart of Catholic education.

Educating in a Catholic school provides both a unique opportunity and a complex challenge. The Catholic school has a distinct identity that is rooted in the Catholic faith and shaped by the values and vision of the Catholic Church. Teaching in a Catholic school means working in an institution that is shaped by that vision. It means educating students in such a way that they are inspired to live by the values and virtues of the Catholic tradition.

An integral part of Catholic identity is the Church's social teaching. This teaching is at the heart of the Church's mission and, therefore, at the heart of Catholic education. It is a tradition that offers a unique and challenging vision of how to live a dignified life, a life of commitment to the common good, a life dedicated to God's great commandment of love. Educators who are committed to these social values and to helping students live by these values are fulfilling a very special and challenging vocation. They are responding to God's calling as embodied in the words of the prophet Micah: "What does the Lord require of you, but only this — to act justly, to love tenderly, and to walk humbly with your God" (Micah 6:8).

The teachings of the Second Vatican Council are an important source to help clarify the centrality of the Church's social mission. In one of the Council's most important documents, *The Pastoral Constitution on the Church and the Modern World*, the bishops of the world said that the Church is to be "the sign and the safeguard" of the dignity of the human person. They described the Church as a religious institution whose purpose is to help bring about the reign of God in history. This means that, by definition, the Church must be engaged in the world, transforming it on behalf of the principles of justice, human dignity, hope, and love.

The integral role of the Church's social mission was again clearly stated in 1971 by the world synod of bishops. In a statement entitled *Justice in the World*, they declared, "Action on behalf of justice and participation in the transformation of the world fully appear to us as a *constitutive* dimension of the preaching of the Gospel, or, in other words, of the Church's mission for the redemption of the human race and its liberation from every oppressive situation."[4]

Unfortunately, many people do not fully understand this part of the Church's mission. They are not familiar with the basic content of Catholic social teaching; and more fundamentally, they do not adequately recognize that the Church's social mission is at the heart of Catholic identity. The social teaching is essential to Catholicity.

Coming to grips with the social mission of the Church means overcoming the tendency to view faith or religion as a purely private affair. The Catholic faith is inherently a social matter. Yes, there are personal and private dimensions of faith, but there are also social dimensions that require believers to take their faith into the marketplace, into the public arena, into the world at large. Indeed, working for justice in these public arenas is not separate from one's faith. It is the living out of faith. It is a religious act. As Jesuit biblical scholar Rev. John R. Donahue, SJ, has stated, "Engagement in the quest for justice is no more 'secular' than engagement of Yahweh in the history of God's people or the incarnation of Jesus in the world of human suffering."[5]

The centrality of the social mission is an important principle for the whole Church, but it has a special significance for educators in Catholic schools, for they are charged with the responsibility of educating students according to values that reflect a fundamental Catholic identity. One of the key ways to evaluate the success of Catholic schools, then, is observe the students who graduate from these schools. Do they see themselves as having a responsibility to work for justice in the world? Do they understand this to be a part of their Catholic faith? Do they understand the basic principles of Catholic social teaching? Do they have the personal and public skills to be effective agents on behalf of social justice?

By integrating the social teaching principles and the practice of social justice in their institutions, Catholic schools can be effective signs of the Church's social mission. For example, a school that consciously strives to treat employees and students fairly and to involve them in decision making, is engaged with issues in the wider community and encourages service for the poor, trains its students to be good citizens and advocates for justice in the public arena — such a school will be a sign of hope and grace, both for the students and the wider community. It will be a school in which the Catholic identity is clear.

> One of the key ways to evaluate the success of Catholic schools, then, is observe the students who graduate from these schools. Do they see themselves as having a responsibility to work for justice in the world? Do they understand this to be a part of their Catholic faith?

The tradition of Catholic social thought is a rich resource for Catholic educators. It is a social vision that is rooted in the Bible and shaped by the experience of human history and the wisdom of human reason. This social vision can be an inspiring source of meaning for teachers in Catholic schools and for the students whose lives they help to shape. Of course, while many students and teachers in Catholic schools are themselves members of the Catholic Church, many others are not. Whatever one's own personal religious beliefs are, all who study and work in Catholic schools can appreciate and benefit from the rich values of Catholic social teaching because this teaching promotes a social vision that appeals to the deepest, most authentic human striving for dignity and justice. It is a vision that is key to Catholic identity. It is this vision that that can enrich Catholic education.

Chapter 2

Biblical Foundations
of Catholic Social Teaching

E ducators who wish to enrich their teaching with the values of
Catholic social teaching would do well to begin by studying
and reflecting on the actual content of this teaching. The present
chapter and the one following provide an introduction to some of
the key themes from that teaching.

Traditionally the Church has drawn on two sources of wisdom in
its teaching about social values. It looks first to the biblical values
found in the Hebrew Scriptures and the New Testament, and it
complements this with a tradition of modern social teaching documents that rely more heavily on rational and philosophical language.
Prime examples of this modern social teaching are the papal encyclicals about social justice. These two sources — Scripture and tradition — combine to form a unified body of wisdom that can help
modern day Christians live faith-filled and grace-filled lives.

The Sacred Scriptures are inherently a teaching about justice. This chapter highlights seven key themes from the Bible that shape the Christian vision of social life. This brief summary is not a substitute for a more extended and thorough study of the scriptural roots of social justice. However, by highlighting some examples of the key themes, it can serve to demonstrate the richness of the Catholic social vision and the importance of making this vision an integral part of contemporary Catholic education.

GOD OF JUSTICE

At the heart of the Hebrew Scriptures is an understanding of God as the God of justice and righteousness. God is understood as One who is actively involved in human history, a God who cares passionately about the people of Israel and who intervenes on their behalf. As the scriptures say, God "is a God of justice" (Is. 30:18) who "secures justice and the rights of all the oppressed" (Ps. 103:6). God hates injustice (Is. 61:8) and rejoices when justice is realized (Jer. 9:24).

In the biblical tradition, justice is a fundamental mandate because God is just and those in covenant with God must live justly and work for justice in the community. For the Hebrew faith, to ignore the demands of justice or to forget that justice is central to the covenant is considered to be a form of blasphemy. For the devout Jew of ancient times, the doing of justice is at the heart of faith. Donohue points out that in the Hebrew Scriptures "the doing of justice is not the application of religious faith, but its substance; without it, God remains unknown."[6]

It should be noted that this emphasis on justice in the Bible is not unique to the Catholic tradition, but is shared by many in the Protestant and Jewish communities. Thus, for example, the renowned Hebrew Scripture scholar Walter Brueggemann writes, "In biblical faith, the doing of justice is the primary expectation of God."[7] Similarly, G. von Rad writes, "There is absolutely no concept in the Old Testament with so central for all relationships of human life as that of *sedaqah* [justice/righteousness]."[8]

The biblical concept of justice has a meaning that is deeper and more encompassing than the secular or philosophical definition that we are accustomed to hearing in contemporary discourse. In its simplest form, this philosophical definition of *just* is "that which is due." It is symbolized by a blindfolded judge balancing a scale to measure what is deserved by each party or what is due to them.

In contrast, the biblical meaning of justice can be described as "fidelity to the demands of right relationships."[9] Rev. Walter Burghardt, SJ explains this definition eloquently when he writes, "When are people just? When they are in right relationship to their God, to their sisters and brothers, to the whole of created reality. When God declared all of creation "very good," it was because simply everything was in right order, in proper relation; humanity to God, humans among themselves, humans and non-human reality toward one another. Justice has to do with the right ordering of all relationships, and so it is central to all of human living."[10]

It should be noted that this concept of justice goes beyond the idea of "giving everyone his due." It adds the great Christian commandment of love based on the idea that God's relationship with humankind should be the model for our relationships with each other. God relates to human beings, not as a blindfolded, neutral, judge, but as one who feels compassion, mercy, and loving kindness. Biblical justice, then, is justice with compassion. It is a justice that is overflowing with love, especially for those who are poor, weak, or oppressed.

CREATION

From the very first chapter of the book of Genesis, the Bible conveys a powerful message about creation. All of the goods of the earth are a gift from God, and this is a gift that is meant for the use of all, not for the private exploitation of a few. God created all things, and at the pinnacle of creation God created the human person, made in God's image and likeness. For this reason, we say that there is a piece of the sacred in human beings. They share a special human dignity that flows from God and is inherent in their being.

The book of Genesis presents a story in which God carefully constructs the universe. The author poetically pictures God dealing with the universe like a child in a sandbox. He draws lines and the rivers are created. He tosses the stars into the heavens and separates the waters. He holds the world in his hand the way a child holds the ball of sand. With this imagery, the story reminds us of the grandeur of creation, the overwhelming wonder of what God has made. And then, the story tells us, when the world was created, God made human beings in His image. The human person is placed at the pinnacle of creation, and the world and all that is in it is put at the service of the person.

The creation stories of the Bible also contain important lessons about stewardship. Stewardship means more than the fact that creation is a gift and that human beings are to guard over what God has made. The full meaning of stewardship is that human beings share in a very real way in the ongoing development and fulfillment of the creative process that God began in the story of Genesis.

Our task as faithful stewards is to carry on the work of creation that God began. We are to bring this work to fulfillment. In this sense, we are "co-creators" with God. We share in God's creative work. We participate in the ongoing work of creation.

From the biblical perspective, human history is future-directed. Men and women are charged with the responsibility of helping to build the kingdom of God, a kingdom whose full dimensions are not yet completely realized. In carrying out this responsibility, human beings do God's work. They share in God's continuing work of creation. Thus when Christians pray, "Thy kingdom come, they will be done on earth as it is in heaven," they are committing themselves to active engagement in the world so that God's kingdom will be realized here on earth, so that God's will may be done here and now.

COVENANT

At the heart of God's relationship to the people of Israel was the covenant. God said, "I will be your God and you will be my people." This special relationship was embodied in the covenant, and everyone knew the responsibilities and expectations that were implied in the covenant. Those who participated in this relationship understood that justice was an integral part of the covenant. To be in covenant with the God of justice meant that they too had to be just and to seek justice. They knew themselves as a covenant people, a people called to shape a community of justice.

Living justly and keeping the covenant, then, were part and parcel of the same relationship. It meant that people were to live in right relationship with God, self, others, and creation. As noted earlier, this "fidelity to the demands of right relationships" is the biblical definition of justice.

Author and educator Dr. Thomas Groome reiterates that this covenant relationship, this living according to the demands of justice, means more than scrupulously "weighing the scales" and determining what is due to others in strictly ethical terms. In Dr. Groome's words, "A covenant kind of 'right relationship' gives what is due and then 'flows over' like a gentle rain."[11]

> There are few words that characterize the message of the Hebrew Scriptures more accurately than community. The story of the people of Israel is, at its roots, a story about a communal people.

Closely related to the idea of covenant is the theme of community. There are few words that characterize the message of the Hebrew Scriptures more accurately than community. The story of the people of Israel is, at its roots, a story about a communal people. They understood themselves to be social beings, not isolated individuals. They understood salvation in a communal sense because God related to them as a covenant people, not as individual believers.

Faithfulness to God, then, implies significant social responsibilities because God's will is realized in and through social institutions, political structures, and all of the complex human constructs that make up society. Those who make a covenant with God commit themselves to working for justice within those institutions and structures.

EXODUS

The God of the Hebrew Scriptures is a God who gives life, who acts with mercy and compassion. God forgives, liberates, and often rescues the covenant people from disaster. Perhaps the most dramatic example in the Bible is the exodus event in which a compassionate God brought the people out of the oppression of slavery to freedom in a land flowing with milk and honey. God told Moses, "I have observed the misery of my people who are in Egypt; I have heard their cry on account of their taskmasters. Indeed, I know their sufferings…" (Ex. 3:7-8). In an act that is symbolic of all of God's actions, God was moved by compassion and the people were set free. God always moves people from slavery to a state of freedom.

The people who were in covenant with God were expected to act as God acted — with compassion, with acts of forgiveness, and setting others free. They were to follow God's example by treating the alien and the slave in their midst as God had treated them (Ex. 22:20-22). They were to direct their lives according to God's will, which was understood to be embodied in Israel's great legal codes such as the Decalogue (Ex. 20:1-17) and the Book of the Covenant (Ex. 20:22-23:33). These codes made life in community possible. Included in these laws was the expectation that all members of the community should manifest a special concern for the vulnerable members of the community: widows, orphans, the poor, and strangers in the land.

The Poor

Throughout the Bible, God is revealed as one who cares in a special way for the poor. God came to the aid of the oppressed and enslaved people and formed them into a covenant community. One of the primary expectations of this community was that the people take care of the "anawim," the "little ones."

The people knew that their God had a special love for the poor, for those who were powerless. They also knew that, as people of the covenant, they were to imitate God's special love for the poor. As God does, so should God's people do.[12]

The U.S. bishops summarized the biblical emphasis on the poor when they wrote in *Economic Justice for All*:

> *Central to the biblical presentation of justice is that the justice of a community is measured by its treatment of the powerless in society, most often described as the widow, the orphan, the poor, and the*

stranger (non-Israelite) in the land. The Law, the Prophets, and the
Wisdom literature of the Old Testament all show deep concern for
the proper treatment of such people. What these groups of people have
in common is their vulnerability and lack of power. They are often
alone and have no protector or advocate. Therefore, it is God who
hears their cries (Ps. 109:21; 113:7).[13]

Throughout the Hebrew Scriptures, the phrase "widows, orphans, and aliens" is used as a shorthand way of referring to all those who are poor and weak. Therefore, the ultimate test of whether the community was living justly was to look and see how well the widows, orphans, and aliens were being treated. If these "little ones" were not being treated fairly, then the people knew that their relationships were not in right order. Justice was not present. The covenant was not being upheld. Yahweh was not pleased.

THE PROPHETS

Throughout the Bible, the prophets are central figures. They appeared among the people from time to time to remind them of the demands that flow from the covenant. They recalled for the people the basic truth that their relationship with Yahweh was to be judged by the quality of justice that was found in their community and that justice was to be measured by how well the widows, orphans, and aliens were being treated.

Repeatedly the people forgot this basic truth. They fell back to the pre-Exodus notion of religion in which worship and ritual were believed to be the primary duty of the faithful person. Repeatedly the prophets came to remind them that social responsibility, the doing of justice, was a key to their relationship with God. One can almost picture the prophet arriving on the scene just as the priests are getting everyone to the temple to pray and offer incense. The prophet shows up at the door and says, in effect, "Let me tell you about your faith. Let me tell you what kind of worship your God expects." Thus we read the famous words of Isaiah 58: "Is this the manner of fasting I wish, of keeping a day of penance: That a man bow his head like a reed, and lie in sackcloth and ashes? Do you call this a fast, a day acceptable to the Lord? This, rather, is the fasting that I wish: releasing those bound unjustly, untying the thongs of the yoke; setting free the oppressed, breaking every yoke…" (Is. 58:5-6).

The classic biblical statement of what God expects of believers is found in Micah 6:8. This text is considered by many biblical experts to be a concise summary of the whole prophetic tradition. As Dr. Groome explains, the beginning of the sixth chapter of Micah is a dramatic passage in which Yahweh puts Israel on trial for "forgetting" — forgetting that Yahweh had set them free from slavery and liberated them from oppression. They had forgotten what this liberating God expected of them as part of the covenant. Israel tries to plea-bargain and offers to increase is sacrificial offerings. "But then," writes Groome, "in the climactic punch line of Micah 6:8, Yahweh looks out over the head of Israel and addresses all humankind, saying 'This is what Yahweh asks of you, oh humankind: only this, to act justly, to love tenderly, and to walk humbly with your God.'"[14]

Throughout the Scriptures, this message remains constant. Whether the prophet was Micah, Isaiah, Jeremiah, any of the others, they all proclaimed the same truth — that the covenant of right relationship demanded a faith that does justice with love.

THE EXAMPLE OF JESUS

In the New Testament, Jesus repeated and reinforced the message of the Hebrew Scriptures. By His words and deeds, He proclaimed that the faithful should seek to imitate God. Just as God set the people free from slavery, so must believers in every age work to set free those who are in bondage, those who are oppressed. No one who worships the God of Exodus can rest easily in the face of human misery and suffering.

In his first public utterance, Jesus stood up in the synagogue and unrolled the scroll. The passage He chose to read says a lot about the message that He came to preach. We read in the Gospel of Luke that:

> *He opened the book, and found the place where it was written, "The Spirit of the Lord is upon me, because he anointed me to preach good tidings to the poor: He hath sent me to proclaim release to the captives, and recovering of sight to the blind, to set at liberty them that are bruised, to proclaim the acceptable year of the Lord." And he*

closed the book, and sat down, and the eyes of all in the synagogue were fastened on him. And he began to say unto them, "Today this scripture has been fulfilled in your ears" (Lk. 4:17-21).

Jesus always showed a special favor for the poor, the outcasts, and the weak. He associated with prostitutes, tax collectors, lepers, and foreigners. In the Beatitudes, He said that the reign of God belongs to the poor and he promised satisfaction to those who work for justice. And in a somewhat shocking description of the final judgment day, He said that the King will condemn those who fail to respond to the needs of the poor, the hungry, those in prison, and those who are oppressed. As Jesus said in Matthew 25:40, "The King will answer and say to them, 'Truly I say to you, to the extent that you did it to one of these brothers of Mine, even the least of them, you did it to Me... Depart from Me, accursed ones, into the eternal fire which has been prepared for the devil and his angels.'"

In the end, what Jesus preached was a new commandment of love, a love that was radical and demanding. "You shall love your neighbor as yourself." No longer were His followers to use the principle "an eye for an eye and a tooth for a tooth." Rather, Jesus said, "Love your enemies." For Jesus, love was a commandment, a duty. It was and is no longer a matter of doing my neighbor a favor out of the generosity of my heart. Rather, true love is a matter of giving people what is owed to them. It is a matter of restoring right relationships. It is a matter of justice.

> For Jesus, love was a commandment, a duty. It was and is no longer a matter of doing my neighbor a favor out of the generosity of my heart. Rather, true love is a matter of giving people what I owe them. It is a matter of restoring right relationships. It is a matter of justice.

The Acts of the Apostles and the epistles of Paul also lift up and reinforce key themes of justice and liberation found in the Bible. In the Acts of the Apostles, the early Christians understood themselves to be members of a new community. They were "God's own people" (1 Pt. 2:9-10), who, like the people of Exodus, owed their existence to God's compassion and liberation. They believed that they walked in the newness of life (Rom. 6:4), that the old creation had passed away and the new had come (2 Cor. 5:17).

In attempting to follow the example of Jesus and to live in the newness of life, the early Christians had a very strong commitment to community. We are told that they distributed their possessions so that "there was no needy person among them," and that they held "all things in common" (Acts 4:32-34; 2:44). Another powerful example is found in Paul's letter to the Corinthians. He uses the image of the body to convey the importance of community. "We are all members of one body... When one member of the body suffers, all suffer as one" (I Cor. 12:12,26).

The themes listed above are but a sampling of the rich message of justice, compassion, and liberation that is found in the Bible. These biblical foundations of social justice form the basis for the modern tradition of Catholic social teaching which will be explored in the next chapter. They also express a strong challenge to us as individuals and as professional educators. They call us to act on behalf of justice in our world, firm in the conviction that, despite the power of injustice, life has been fundamentally changed by God's Incarnation into human history.

Chapter 3

A Summary of Modern Catholic Social Teaching

The joys and the hopes, the griefs and the anxieties of the people of this age, especially those who are poor or in any way afflicted, these are the joys and hopes, the griefs and anxieties of the followers of Christ.

— Second Vatican Council [15]

These famous words from the Second Vatican Council point to a very basic challenge that all Christians face — how does one act in the world in a way that is true to the Gospel? How does one live a responsible and faith-filled life in the face of a complicated and changing world? How does one act justly and carry out the Church's social mission in the modern world?

That is the question taken up by Catholic social teaching. This teaching is embodied in the papal encyclicals and official documents that have been issued by the Church on topics related to social justice. The modern body of social teaching during the last century takes the biblical themes of justice and develops them in a

19

more specific way. It systematizes and deepens the wisdom from the biblical tradition. It uses contemporary philosophical language to interpret the social teaching, and it applies the teaching in more specific ways to the historical realities of our time.

In the Catholic tradition, the followers of Christ are not expected to live completely apart from the world; rather, they are to engage it and transform it. In carrying out this challenge, the Church draws on the moral wisdom that is embodied in both faith and reason. By faith, one knows that the word of God is revealed in the Bible. By using human reason, one is able to reflect on nature and human experience in a way that helps one to make ethical choices. Faith and reason, then, are complementary.

Some Catholic theologians have used the phrase "the Catholic and" to emphasize this notion that the Catholic vision of reality is complementary, not contradictory. This tradition speaks of *faith* and *reason, grace* and *nature, Church* and *world, altar* and *marketplace*. In other words, faith goes beyond reason, but does not contradict it. Grace perfects nature, it does not destroy it. The Church is called to transform the world, not retreat from it. Prayer around the altar is intended to send the faithful into the marketplace, not remove them from it.

Modern Catholic social teaching, then, is a body of wisdom that can help us live justly in the contemporary world. Starting with Pope Leo XIII's encyclical *Rerum Novarum* in 1891 and continuing through to the most recent documents of Pope John Paul II, the social teaching documents constitute a growing and developing tradition. Together, these documents suggest a Christian social vision, a particular way of looking at the world. As Rev. Bryan Hehir has suggested, this teaching can help the Church to shape a "community of conscience," a body of believers whose character and social values are shaped by the principles of justice.

While some aspects of Catholic encyclicals have changed over the last century to reflect the changes in historical circumstances, the underlying moral principles have remained consistent. The remainder of this chapter summarizes these key principles under ten themes. This list is a somewhat expanded version of the seven key themes listed in the U.S. bishops 1998 statement, *Sharing Catholic Social Teaching: Challenges and Directions*. While the list presented here is not, in any way, an official or comprehensive list, it does reflect the major principles that are central to Catholic social teaching. Following each theme are passages from Church documents that address the given theme.

HUMAN DIGNITY

The Catholic Church proclaims that human life is sacred and that the dignity of the human person is the foundation of a moral vision for society. Our belief in the sanctity of human life and the inherent dignity of the human person is the foundation of all the principles of our social teaching.[16]

There is no more basic principle in the Catholic social vision than the dignity of the human person. It is the bedrock theme, the place where the Church stands when it addresses the question of justice in the world. In the words of the Second Vatican Council, the Church is "the sign and the safeguard of the transcendental dimension of the human person."[17]

> There is no more basic principle in the Catholic social vision than the dignity of the human person. It is the bedrock theme, the place where the Church stands when it addresses the question of justice in the world.

We are required to honor the human person, to give priority to the person because of the intrinsic dignity that each person possesses. Philosophically, we can understand that human persons have special status because of their ability to make free choices, their capacity for love, self-reflection, and knowledge. These characteristics set the human person apart from the rest of creation.

Theologically, the principle of human dignity is grounded in the idea that the person is sacred, made in the image of God. The person is the clearest reflection of God among us. As the bishops said in their 1986 pastoral letter on the economy, every person "must be respected with a reverence that is religious. When we deal with each other, we should do so with the sense of awe that arises in the presence of something holy and sacred."[18] In other words, when we look into the eyes of the human person, we see there the greatest manifestation of the grandeur of God, the clearest reflection of the presence of God among us.

We are asked never to forget this most basic principle: people are more important than things. Every person, regardless of age, sex, race, gender, religion, or economic status, has the special dignity that comes from being a child of God. Every person is a reflection of the sacred and is worthy of respect.

Passages

Whatever insults human dignity, such as subhuman living conditions, arbitrary imprisonment, deportation, slavery, prostitution...as well as disgraceful working conditions, where people are treated as mere tools for profit, rather than as free and responsible persons; all these things and others of their like are infamies indeed. They poison human society, but they do more harm to those who practice them than those who suffer from the injury (*Pastoral Constitution on the Church in the Modern World, # 27*).

Every perspective on economic life that is human, moral, and Christian must be shaped by three questions: What does the economy do for people? What does it do to people? And how do people participate in it? (*Economic Justice for All, #1*)

Any human society, if it is to be well ordered and productive, must lay down as a foundation this principle, namely, that every human being is a person, that is, his or her nature is endowed with intelligence and free will. Indeed, precisely because he or she is a person, he or she has rights and obligations flowing directly and simultaneously from his or her very nature (*Peace on Earth, #9*).

The basis for all that the Church believes about the moral dimensions of economic life is its vision of the transcendent worth — the sacredness — of human beings. The dignity of the human person, realized in community with others, is the criterion against which all aspects of economic life must be measured (*Economic Justice for All, #28*). ■

COMMUNITY AND THE COMMON GOOD

In Catholic social thought, the person is not only sacred but also social. The very nature of human beings is that they are communal creatures. They live and grow in community. They cannot survive without community. Therefore, the dignity of the person makes sense only in the context of the person's relationships to others in the community. Human dignity can only be realized and protected in the context of relationships with society.

This principle has profound implications not only for individual attitudes and behavior, but also for the institutions and structures of society. How we organize society — economically, politically, legally — directly affects human dignity and the capacity of individuals to grow in community. The obligation to "love our neighbor," therefore, has an individual dimension, but it also requires a broader social commitment to the common good. Everyone has an obligation to contribute to the good of the whole society, to the common good. If we are serious about our commitment to the dignity of the human person, we must be serious about humanizing the social systems in which the person lives.

> The common good grows out of the social nature of the human person and is defined as the sum total of spiritual, material, and social conditions that are necessary in order that all in society might realize their full human dignity.

This is a difficult truth to be taught — particularly in our culture and our time, when individualism is a dominant and sometimes rampant cultural force. Contemporary society is characterized by a radical separation of private life and social life. Far too often, American culture promotes an ethic of private interest and private struggle to the near exclusion of social virtues and social commitments. The nation is witnessing a loss of commitment to the social order, a declining willingness to sacrifice one's immediate selfish interests for the good of the wider society. This radically privatized, radically individualized culture operates on a creed that Charles Dickens once described in the following way: "'Every man for himself,' said the elephant, as he danced among the chickens."

In the face of this rampant individualism, Catholic social teaching insists that we are all radically social. It promotes a vision in which community plays a central role. As the Apostle Paul wrote the Corinthians:

> *The body is one and has many members, but all the members, many though they are, are one body; and so it is with Christ. It is in one Spirit that all of us, whether Jew or Greek, slave or free, were baptized into one body...If one member suffers, all the members suffer with it; if one member is honored, all the members share its joy. You, then, are the body of Christ. Every one of you is a member of it (I Cor. 12:12-27).*

The notion of the common good plays a central role in the Catholic vision of social life. The common good grows out of the social nature of the human person and is defined as the sum total of spiritual, material, and social conditions that are necessary in order that all in society might realize their full human dignity. All of society is responsible for contributing to the common good, and by doing so, they enhance their own dignity. In view of the excessive individualism in our culture, it can be argued that restoring a healthy commitment to the common good is one of the most significant social tasks of our time.

Passages

The common good embraces the sum total of all those conditions of social life which enable individuals, families, and organizations to achieve complete and effective fulfillment *(Mother and Teacher, #74).*

It is imperative that no one...would indulge in a merely individualistic morality. The best way to fulfill one's obligations of justice and love is to contribute to the common good according to one's means and the needs of others, and also to promote and help public and private organizations devoted to bettering the conditions of life *(Pastoral Constitution on the Church in the Modern World, # 30).*

It is demanded by the common good that civil authorities should make earnest efforts to bring about a situation in which individual citizens can easily exercise their rights and fulfill their duties as well. For experience has taught us that, unless these authorities take suitable action with regard to economic, political, and cultural matters, inequalities between the citizens tend to become more and more widespread, especially in the modern world, and as a result, human rights are rendered totally ineffective and the fulfillment of duties is compromised *(Peace on Earth, #63).* ■

RIGHTS AND RESPONSIBILITIES

In Catholic social teaching, the basic demands of justice are made explicit by a specific set of human rights. These rights are bestowed on human beings by God and grounded in the nature and dignity of the person. They are not created by society, but rather, are inherent in the very nature of every person. These fundamental rights form a kind of baseline, a set of minimum conditions for social justice. They form a bottom line for judging how well society's institutions are protecting human dignity.

A "right" as presented in Catholic teaching is a moral claim that is based on one's dignity. These moral claims are of two types. The first are civil and political rights, such as freedom of speech, freedom of assembly, and the other rights protected by the Constitution of the United States. These rights are a form of immunity from unjust interference. They imply a moral claim against others in society, preventing them from unnecessarily limiting one's basic freedoms.

A second category of rights consists of economic rights, such as food and shelter. These are rights that might be thought of as "empowerments." They are claims made on others in society for specific goods that enable people to realize their full human dignity. In Catholic teaching, economic rights include, above all, the basic material necessities that are required to live decently. As the U.S. bishops state in their pastoral letter on the economy:

> First among these are the rights to life, food, clothing, shelter, rest, medical care, and basic education. These are indispensable to the protection of human dignity. In order to ensure these necessities, all persons have a right to earn a living, which for most people in our economy is through remunerative employment.[19]

Human rights, then, are the minimum conditions for life in the community. When people are hungry and homeless, when they do not have access to health care or employment, they are being denied basic rights. Society, therefore, must ensure that these rights are protected.

In Catholic teaching, the concept of human rights is closely tied to that of responsibilities. Corresponding to the basic rights enjoyed by all people are fundamental duties and responsibilities — to one another, to families, and to the larger society. For example, people have a right to adequate employment, but they also have a duty to work and a responsibility to provide adequate income for their families. Moreover, the wider society also has a responsibility to organize its economic structures so that the right to employment is protected for all. Without this collective social responsibility being fulfilled, an individual's right to employment would have little practical meaning.

Public debate in our nation is often divided between those who focus on personal responsibility and those who focus on social responsibilities. As the above discussion points out, the Catholic tradition insists that both personal and social responsibilities are necessary. As a nation, we are challenged to ask a basic question — how can we structure society so that we guarantee that no one goes without the basic goods that are essential to human dignity?

While the concept of human rights may sound rather straightforward and basic, it is one of the more controversial ideas in Catholic social teaching, especially when the rights in question are economic in nature. Our society understands civil and political rights, and there is a political consensus that supports these rights. As a result, the nation has put in place social policies and structures that protect these rights, and punish those who violate these rights.

In contrast, society has a very different attitude toward rights that are economic in nature. Indeed many Americans disagree with the very idea of economic rights. The nation does not have a consensus in support of these rights, nor does it have in place the kinds of policies and structures that are needed to adequately protect these rights. One of the Church's important educational tasks, therefore, is to help build a broader consensus that the basic economic conditions of human welfare are essential to human dignity and are due by right.

Passages

Everyone has the right to life, to bodily integrity, and to the means which are suitable for the proper development of life; these are primarily food, clothing, shelter, rest, medical care, and finally the necessary social services. Therefore, a human being also has the right to security in cases of sickness, inability to work, widowhood, old age, unemployment, or in any other case in which one is deprived of the means of subsistence through no fault of one's own *(Peace on Earth, #11)*.

Those, therefore, who claim their own rights, yet altogether forget or neglect to carry out their respective duties, are people who build with one hand and destroy with the other. Since people are social by nature, they are meant to live with others and to work for one another's welfare...A well-ordered human society requires that people recognize and observe their mutual rights and duties. It also demands that each contribute generously to the establishment of a civic order in which rights and duties are more sincerely and effectively acknowledged and fulfilled *(Peace on Earth #30-31)*.

These fundamental personal rights — civil and political as well as social and economic — state the minimum conditions for social institutions that respect human dignity, social solidarity, and justice. They are all essential to human dignity and to the integral development of both individuals and society, and are thus moral issues. Any denial of these rights harms persons and wounds the human community. Their serious and sustained denial violates individuals and destroys solidarity among persons *(Economic Justice for All, #80)*. ■

OPTION FOR THE POOR

The theme of special care and love for the poor is one that is central to the biblical notion of justice. The Hebrew Scriptures emphasize that God expects those who are faithful to the covenant to pay special attention to the "widows, orphans, and aliens." Indeed, the treatment of the poor was one of the bottom-line tests of the people's faith in Yahweh. In the New Testament, Jesus recalled and carried on this theme. In the Beatitudes, in the story of the last judgment (Mt. 25), and in the whole of Jesus' life and teaching, it is unmistakably clear that those who seek to follow the way of Jesus must care for the poor in a special way.

In contemporary times, the Church has adopted the phrase "option for the poor" to describe this moral principle. Pope John Paul II has spoken of this special obligation to the poor as "a preferential, but not exclusive, love of the poor." He has described this preferential love as a "call to have a special openness with the small and the weak, those that suffer and weep, those that are humiliated and left on the margin of society, so as to help them win their dignity as human persons and children of God."[20]

It is important to note that the word "option" here implies a special preference for the poor and the weak, but it is not intended to be a theme that is, in any way, divisive. It does not mean that one should opt for the poor and against those who are not poor. The U.S. bishops make this point in their pastoral letter on the economy when they write:

> *The primary purpose of this special commitment to the poor is to enable them to become active participants in the life of society. It is to enable all persons to share in and contribute to the common good. The "option for the poor," therefore, is not an adversarial slogan that pits one group or class against another. Rather it states that the deprivation and powerlessness of the poor wounds the whole community.[21]*

While this moral theme obviously has strong implications for one's individual actions and one's personal life, it also has great importance at a social and structural level. The bishops' pastoral letter is emphatic on this point. They declare that, "As individuals and as a nation, we are called to make a fundamental 'option for the poor'. The obligation to evaluate social and economic activity from the viewpoint of the poor and the powerless arises from the radical command to love one's neighbor as one's self. Those who are marginalized and whose rights are denied have privileged claims if society is to provide justice for all."[22]

The "preference" or "option" for the poor, then, gives Catholics a certain angle of vision, a way of looking at society that has a bias in favor of the weak and powerless. It is a perspective that examines personal decisions, policies of private and public bodies, and power relationships in terms of their effects on the poor — those who lack the minimum necessities of nutrition, housing, education, and health care.

This moral principle is closely tied to the values of human dignity and community. In light of the social nature of the person, Catholics believe that human dignity can only be fully realized in a community. A healthy community, in turn, can be achieved only if its members give special attention to those with special needs, to those who are poor and on the margins of society. Just as a family with a handicapped child cannot function in a healthy and mature way unless its members give special attention to that child, so a society cannot function well unless the poor get special attention. And just like the family with a handicapped child, if the members follow this principle, the beneficiaries are not only the handicapped and the needy but everyone. All members of the family or the society are better off. It follows, then, that the "option for the poor" is an essential part of society's effort to achieve the common good.

Passages

In teaching us charity, the Gospel instructs us in the preferential respect due to the poor and the special situation they have in society: the more fortunate should renounce some of their rights so as to place their goods more generously at the service of others *(A Call to Action, #23)*.

A consistent theme of Catholic social teaching is the option or love of preference for the poor. Today, this preference has to be expressed in worldwide dimensions, embracing the immense numbers of the hungry, the needy, the homeless, those without medical care, and those without hope *(On Social Concern, #42)*.

As individuals and as a nation, therefore, we are called to make a fundamental "option for the poor". The obligation to evaluate social and economic activity from the viewpoint of the poor and the powerless arises from the radical command to love one's neighbor as one's self. Those who are marginalized and whose rights are denied have privileged claims if society is to provide justice for all. This obligation is deeply rooted in Christian belief *(Economic Justice for All, #87)*.

It is well known how strong the words were used by the Fathers of the Church to describe the proper attitude of persons who possess anything towards persons in need. To quote Saint Ambrose: "You are not making a gift of your possessions to the poor person. You are handing over to him what is his. For what has been given in common for the use of all, you have arrogated to yourself. The world is given to all, and not only to the rich" *(On the Development of Peoples, #23).* ■

PARTICIPATION

Flowing from the principles of dignity and community is the theme of participation. Catholic social teaching emphasizes the belief that all people have a right to participate in the economic, political, and cultural life of society. It is a fundamental demand of justice and a requirement for human dignity that all people be assured of a minimum level of participation in the community. Conversely, it is wrong for a person or a group to be excluded unfairly or to be unable to participate or contribute to society. In the words of the U.S. bishops, "The ultimate injustice is for a person or group to be treated actively or abandoned passively as if they were nonmembers of the human race. To treat people this way is effectively to say they simply do not count as human beings."[23]

There are both rights and responsibilities associated with this principle. For example, in the political arena, people have a right to participate in the decisions that affect their lives, but they also have a responsibility to contribute, to take advantage of the opportunities to participate in the political process. One might use this principle to reflect on the current state of politics in the United States. Many people are alienated from the political process and frustrated with a campaign financing system that gives far greater access to wealthy contributors. The principle of participation would suggest that this system is not just. It needs reform. At the same time, this moral principle implies that individual citizens have the duty to use the tools of the democracy to reform the system and to make it more accountable and responsible to everyone. Thus, there are not only structural and systemic implications of this principle, but also individual and personal implications.

The right to participate can also be seriously violated in the economic realm. For example, many individuals and families fall victim to the downward cycle of poverty that is caused by economic factors which they are powerless to control. The economic forces of the marketplace do not automatically protect everyone's right to participate. As a result, the poor, the unemployed, and the disabled often get left behind.

This pattern of exclusion is also evident at the international level. Entire nations are blocked from fully participating in the global economy because they lack the economic and political power to change their disadvantaged position. Some of the poorest nations, for example, are saddled with massive international debt repayments that make it virtually impossible for them to pursue fundamental economic development for their own people.

Passages

All people have a right to participate in the economic life of society. Basic justice demands that people be assured a minimum level of participation in the economy. It is wrong for a person or a group to be excluded unfairly or to be unable to participate or contribute to the economy *(Economic Justice for All, #15).*

The principle of participation leads us to the conviction that the most appropriate and fundamental solutions to poverty will be those that enable people to take control of their own lives. For poverty is not merely the lack of financial resources. It entails a more profound kind of deprivation, a denial of full participation in the economic, social, and political life of society and an inability to influence decisions that affect one's life. It means being powerless in a way that assaults not only one's pocketbook but also one's fundamental human dignity *(Economic Justice for All, #188).*

It is fully in accord with human nature that politico-juridical structures be devised which will increasingly and without discrimination provide all citizens with effective opportunities to play a free, active part in the establishment of the juridical foundations of the political community, in the administration of public affairs, in the determining the aims and the terms of reference of public bodies, and in the election of political leaders. All citizens ought to be aware of their

right and duty to promote the common good by casting their votes
(Pastoral Constitution on the Church in the Modern World, #75). ■

WORK AND THE RIGHTS OF WORKERS

Work has a special significance in the Catholic tradition because,
as the creation ethic in Genesis teaches, we have a responsibility to
carry forward God's creative activity. Work is a primary way in which
we do that. When we work, we are carrying out our role as co-
creators with God in the ongoing saga of creation. As the U.S. bishops have said, "Work is more than a way to make a living; it is a
form of continuing participation in God's creation. If the dignity of
work is to be protected, then the basic rights of workers must be
respected—the right to productive work, to decent and fair wages,
to organize and join unions, to private property, and to economic
initiative."[24]

This topic is closely related to the theme of participation discussed above. Work is a form of participation that is vital to human
development because it is through work that most people meet
their basic material needs and exercise their talents. People who are
able and willing to work, but cannot get a job, are deprived of a
chance to participate and to contribute to the economy and to the
good of society.

Catholic encyclical documents have given a great deal of attention to the topic of work and workers rights. This has been an
important theme in many of the papal encyclicals that have been
issued over the past century, and in 1981 Pope John Paul II issued
an entire document on this subject, entitled *On Human Work*. The
Pope emphasized that work has a special dignity because it is performed by the human person. It is a primary way in which the
person becomes fully human and participates in society.

Workers have a right to participate in the decisions that affect
them, and the normal way in which they exercise this right is through
collective bargaining. Catholic teaching holds that all workers have
a right to form unions as a means of protecting their rights and
participating in decisions that affect the workplace. Pope John Paul
II not only affirms this right in his encyclical letter, but he also says

that unions are an "indispensable" element in the search for social justice. He points out that workers and their unions have basic rights that must be safeguarded, but they also have a duty to promote the common good.

Passages

Work remains a good thing, not only because it is useful and enjoyable, but also because it expresses and increases the worker's dignity. Through work, we not only transform the world, we are transformed ourselves, becoming "more a human being" *(On Human Work, #9)*.

Human work is the key to the solution...of the whole "social question." To consider work is of decisive importance when trying to make life "more human" *(On Human Work, #3)*.

The Church fully supports the right of workers to form unions or other associations to secure their rights to fair wages and working conditions. This is a specific application of the more general right to associate. In the words of Pope John Paul II, "The experience of history teaches that organizations of this type are an indispensable element of social life, especially in modern industrial societies" *(Economic Justice for All, #104)*.

We consider it our duty to reaffirm that the remuneration of work is not something that can be left to the laws of the marketplace; nor should it be a decision left to the will of the more powerful. It must be determined in accordance with justice and equity; which means that workers must be paid a wage which allows them to live a truly human life and to fulfill their family obligations in a worthy manner *(Mother and Teacher, #15)*. ∎

STEWARDSHIP OF CREATION

The Church's teaching about environmental responsibility and stewardship of natural resources is rooted in the message of Genesis — the goods of the earth are gifts from God. We humans are not the ultimate owners of these goods, but rather, the temporary stewards. We are entrusted with the responsibility of caring for these gifts and preserving them for future generations. As the Second Vatican Council stated, "God destined the earth and all it contains for all people and nations so that all created things would be shared fairly by all humankind under the guidance of justice tempered by charity."[25]

How we treat the environment — the air and water, the woodlands and grasslands, the farm fields, and the mineral deposits — is a measure of our stewardship, a sign of our respect for the Creator. We are accountable to the Creator of the universe for how well we preserve and care for the earth and its creatures.

In their statement entitled *Renewing the Earth*, the U.S. bishops describe the kind of attitude that reflects this principle of stewardship. They write, "Dwelling in the presence of God, we begin to experience ourselves as part of creation, as stewards within it, not separate from it. As faithful stewards, fullness of life comes from living responsibly within God's creation."[26]

Passages

God destined the earth and all it contains for all people and nations so that all created things would be shared fairly by all humankind under the guidance of justice tempered by charity (*Pastoral Constitution on the Church in the Modern World, #69*).

Material goods and the way we are developing the use of them should be seen as God's gifts to us. They are meant to bring out in each one of us the image of God. We must never lose sight of how we have been created: from the earth and from the breath of God (*On Social Concern, #29*).

From the patristic period to the present, the Church has affirmed that misuse of the world's resources or appropriation of them by a minority of the world's population betrays the gift of creation since "whatever belongs to God belongs to all" (*Economic Justice for All, #34*).

Private property does not constitute for anyone an absolute and unconditioned right. No one is justified in keeping for his or her exclusive use what he or she does not need, when others lack necessities. In a word, "according to the traditional doctrine as found in the Fathers of the Church and the great theologians, the right to property must never be exercised to the detriment of the common good" (*Peace on Earth, #23*). ■

SOLIDARITY

In today's global village, citizens are increasingly aware of the social and economic problems around the world. Hundreds of millions of children go to bed hungry every night because they live in desperate poverty. Millions more suffer the effects of war, ethnic conflicts, and natural disasters. The disparities between poverty and wealth are so extreme as to be almost overwhelming.

In the face of these "signs of the times," people of faith are confronted with a very basic question: "Am I my brother's keeper?" These words from Genesis have always been troubling and difficult to answer. To what extent are we morally and socially responsible for the fate of others, especially those who are in need? This question is difficult enough when it refers to those who are in one's immediate vicinity. But how does one answer that question when it refers to people a half a world away? Am I supposed to be the "keeper" of my brothers and sisters who live in places I have never seen, who speak language I do not understand, and whose culture is radically foreign to my own?

Church teaching answers this question with a resounding "Yes." In their 1997 statement entitled *Called to Global Solidarity,* the U.S. bishops summed up the Church's teaching on solidarity when they pointed out that American Catholics have a special responsibility. They wrote, "We are members of a universal Church that transcends national boundaries and calls us to live in solidarity and justice with the peoples of the world. We are also citizens of a powerful democracy with enormous influence beyond our borders. As Catholics and Americans we arc uniquely called to global solidarity."[27]

Pope John Paul II has been the Church's leading voice on behalf of global solidarity. In fact, he has called solidarity a virtue. It is the virtue, he says, by which we demonstrate "a firm and persevering determination to commit oneself to the common good...because we are all really responsible for all."[28] The Pope may be using a modern word for this virtue, but he goes back to the Bible to explain the foundation for this virtue. He writes, "Sacred Scripture continually speaks to us of an active commitment to our neighbor and demands of us a shared responsibility for all of humanity. This duty is not limited to one's own family, nation, or state, but extends progressively to all...so no one can consider himself or herself extraneous or indifferent to the lot of another member of the human family."[29]

Passages

Solidarity...is not a feeling of vague compassion or shallow distress at the misfortunes of so many people, both near and far. On the contrary, it is a firm and persevering determination to commit oneself to the common good; that is to say, to the good of all and of each individual, because we are all really responsible for all *(On Social Concern, #34)*.

Solidarity is a Christian virtue. It seeks to go beyond itself to total gratuity, forgiveness, and reconciliation. It leads to a new vision of the unity of humankind, a reflection of God's triune intimate life *(On Social Concern, #40)*.

A world divided into blocs, in which, instead of solidarity, imperialism and exploitation hold sway, can only be a world structured in sin. Those structures of sin are rooted in sins committed by individual persons, who introduced these structures and reinforced them again and again. One can blame selfishness, shortsightedness, mistaken political decisions, and imprudent economic decisions; at the root of the evils that afflict the world there is — in one way or another — sin *(On Social Concern, #36)*.

Interdependence must be transformed into solidarity, grounded on the principle that the goods of creation are meant for all. Avoiding every type of imperialism, the stronger nations must feel responsible for the other nations, based on the equality of all peoples and with respect for the differences *(On Social Concern, #39)*. ∎

The Role of Government

One important implication of the principles of solidarity and the social nature of the person has to do with Catholic teaching regarding the role of government. This teaching says that, because we are social beings, the state is natural to the person. Therefore, the state has a positive moral function. It is an instrument to promote human dignity, protect human rights, and build the common good. Its purpose is to assist citizens in fulfilling their responsibility to others in society. Since, in a large and complex society, these responsibilities cannot adequately be carried out on a one-to-one basis, citizens need the help of the government in fulfilling these responsibilities and promoting the common good.

This does not mean that the government should do everything, or that everything done by governments is good. Nor does it imply that public responsibilities should be carried out by a large centralized bureaucracy. Indeed, Catholic social teaching includes the principle of "subsidiarity." This principle includes two important dimensions.

First, subsidiarity suggests that the functions of government should be performed at the lowest level possible, as long as they can be performed adequately. Decision-making and problem solving should be dealt with as close as possible to the local level of communities and institutions. This principle assumes that social problems are better understood and better addressed by people who are close to the problems themselves. In short, this principle starts with a bias towards decentralization in social organization because this will generally result in more efficient and more effective outcomes. It suggests that mediating institutions such as the family, community groups, small businesses, and neighborhood associations should be fostered as a way to promote more effective problem solving and more local control over decision-making.

The second dimension of the principle of subsidiarity is equally important and frequently overlooked. This part of the principle places an important limiting condition on the first part. It says that, when the social needs in question cannot adequately be met at the lower level, then it is not only necessary, but imperative, that higher levels of government intervene to ensure that rights are protected and the common good is advanced.

One shorthand way to summarize the principle of subsidiarity is the phrase, "Small is beautiful, but big when necessary." In other words, start by going to the lowest level possible, but do not hesitate to go to a higher level of government when it is necessary.

Passages

It is agreed that in our time the common good is chiefly guaranteed when personal rights and duties are maintained. The chief concern of civil authorities must therefore be to ensure that these rights are acknowledged, respected, coordinated with other rights, defended, and promoted so that in this way each one may more easily carry out his duties. For "to safeguard the inviolable rights of the human person and to facilitate the fulfillment of his duties should be the chief duties of every public authority" *(Peace on Earth, #60).*

There are needs and common goods that cannot be satisfied by the market system. It is the task of the state and of all society to defend them. An idolatry of the market alone cannot do all that should be done *(The Hundredth Year, #40).*

The teachings of the Church insist that the government has a moral function: protecting human rights and securing basic justice for all members of the commonwealth. Society as a whole and in all its diversity is responsible for building up the common good. But it is the government's role to guarantee the minimum conditions that make this rich social activity possible, namely, human rights and justice. This obligation also falls on individual citizens as they choose their representatives and participate in shaping public opinion *(Economic Justice for All, #122).*

As for the State, its whole raison d'être is the realization of the common good in the temporal order. It cannot, therefore, hold aloof from economic matters. On the contrary, it must do all in its power to promote the production of a sufficient supply of material goods, "the use of which is necessary for the practice of virtue." It has also the duty to protect the rights of all its people, and particularly of its weaker members, the workers, women, and children. It can never be right for the State to shirk its obligation of working actively for the betterment of the condition of the working person *(Mother and Teacher, #20).* ∎

PROMOTION OF PEACE

Catholic teaching has always understood peace as a positive, action-oriented concept. In the words of Pope John Paul II, "Peace is not just the absence of war. It involves mutual respect and confidence between peoples and nations. It involves collaboration and binding agreements. Like a cathedral, peace must be constructed patiently and with unshakable faith."[30] This means that in an increasingly interdependent world, it takes a conscious effort to build peace if we hope to avoid war.

There is a close relationship in Catholic teaching between peace and justice. Peace is the fruit of justice and is dependent upon right order among human beings. This traditional concept of peace was described by the Second Vatican Council in the following way:

> *Peace is not merely the absence of war. Nor can it be reduced solely to the maintenance of a balance of power between enemies. Nor is it brought about by dictatorship. Instead, it is richly and appropriately called "an enterprise of justice" (Is. 32:17). Peace results from that harmony built into human society by its divine founder and actualized by human beings as they thirst after ever greater justice.*[31]

This vision of peace implies that the building up of peace is a task that requires the commitment of individuals and institutions in a variety of social sectors — political, economic, cultural, military, and legal. The Church as an institution and individual Catholics have an important role to play in advancing the goal of peace through each of these social structures and institutions.

Passages

Because peace, like the kingdom of God itself, is both a divine gift and a human work, the Church should continually pray for the gift and share in the work. We are called to be a Church at the service of peace, precisely because peace is one manifestation of God's word and work in our midst *(The Challenge of Peace, #23)*.

Peace is both a gift of God and a human work. It must be constructed on the basis of central human values: truth, justice, freedom, and love *(The Challenge of Peace, #68)*.

In the words of our Holy Father, we need a "moral about face." The whole world must summon the moral courage and technical means to say "no" to nuclear conflict; "no" to weapons of mass destruction; "no" to an arms race which robs the poor and the vulnerable; and "no" to the moral danger of a nuclear age which places before humankind indefensible choices of constant terror or surrender. Peacemaking is not an optional commitment. It is a requirement of our faith. We are called to be peacemakers, not by some movement of the moment, but by our Lord Jesus. The content and context of our peacemaking is set, not by some political agenda or ideological program, but by the teaching of his Church *(The Challenge of Peace, #333)*. ■

The ten themes or principles that have been outlined above are foundational elements of Catholic social teaching. Together, they constitute a unique and challenging moral vision, a way of seeing the world, a lens through which to interpret realty. For Catholic educators, a key question is this: Can I educate my students and help form their characters in such a way that these principles of Catholic social teaching become second nature to them? Can I send my students into society with a worldview and a set of life-long aspirations that are guided by these principles? Teachers who can do this are "Catholic educators" in the true sense of the phrase.

Part **II**

Resources for Integrating Catholic Social Teaching

Chapter 4

Essential Elements for Integrating Catholic Social Teaching

We call for a renewed commitment to integrate Catholic social teaching into the mainstream of all Catholic educational institutions and programs.

— National Conference of Catholic Bishops[32]

If Catholic social teaching is integral to the mission of the Church and essential for the identity of Catholic education, then it follows that this social teaching should have a defining impact on Catholic schools. This can happen most effectively if the values of Catholic social teaching are integrated into every dimension of the institution.

It is not enough to have Catholic social teaching treated as the assigned specialty of the theology faculty or the campus ministry department. If the insight and inspiration of the Church's teaching on social justice is to become a meaningful part of students' lives, then the spirit of this teaching should infuse every part of the institution.

If this were the case, then all teachers would share in the responsibility to communicate this teaching, whether in the social studies classroom, the technology lab, or the math class. Administrators and other staff would also share in this responsibility, and it would become a self evident part of the school's mission, policies, and activities. It would become part of the spirit and atmosphere of the school.

What would it take to achieve this goal? What are the "essential elements" necessary to fully integrate Catholic social teaching into all aspects of a Catholic secondary school? This question was posed to a group of over twenty Catholic high school teachers who came together as a team to work on integrating Catholic social teaching within their schools. The following ten "essential elements" are based on the work of those teachers.

FACULTY FORMATION AND TRAINING

Perhaps no single activity is more crucial than faculty and staff formation. The rationale behind the Church's social teaching, the content of that teaching, and the methods of communicating this teaching to students are simply unknown to many teachers. Where this is the case, teachers are missing a real opportunity — an opportunity to enrich their own lives and to help shape the values and the life choices of the students in their care.

The key here is to give Catholic social teaching sufficient priority, time, and attention, so that all faculty and staff become familiar with the basic rationale and content of this teaching.

Tackling this challenge is not complicated. School administrators and faculty know how to organize formation and training programs, and they do it all the time on a wide range of subjects. The key here is to give Catholic social teaching sufficient priority, time, and attention, so that all faculty and staff become familiar with the basic rationale and content of this teaching. This basic knowledge would include an understanding of the relationship between Christian faith and the social mission of the Church as well as familiarity with the concept of social justice and the key scriptural stories related to biblical justice. Finally, it would include knowledge of the basic moral principles and values of Catholic social teaching as drawn from the encyclical tradition.

Some of this knowledge can be acquired by introductory reading such as the material in this book and the additional resources in the reading list found in Appendix One. Short in-service programs lasting one half-day or a full day are also useful steps in laying a basic foundation of understanding among faculty and staff.

While these actions may be effective in the short term, experience suggests that they need to be accompanied by more in-depth, long-term strategies that allow faculty and staff to study and reflect on the Church's social teaching in a more detailed and thorough manner. Forming monthly reading and discussion groups among faculty and staff is one way to achieve this goal.

Another option is to arrange for faculty and staff to attend full-scale courses or week-long summer institutes in Catholic social thought. These settings provide an opportunity to assimilate the content in a more substantive way. They also allow the kind of time for reflection and dialogue that is necessary if values of Catholic social teaching are to become an integral part of the teachers' spiritual and personal life.

Providing this kind of in-depth training and formation for faculty members is a strategy that may have to be implemented over a long period of time, but there is no substitute for the kind of conviction and enthusiasm that is evident in teachers when they have had the opportunity to digest, grapple with, and take as their own the social vision of the Catholic teaching on justice. Schools that make a long-range plan to send a few teachers each year for this kind of in-depth training will be rewarded with a strong core of faculty who are motivated and equipped to make the Church's social teaching an integral part of the school in which they work.

Integration into all Classrooms

A second essential element is the need for an explicit strategy to integrate Catholic social teaching into all parts of the curriculum. There is a common tendency to assume that teaching students about the values of Catholic social teaching is the function of the religion or theology faculty. It is easy to say, "Let them handle that material. Why should the math or science teacher worry about Catholic social values?"

To answer that question, it is important to understand Catholic social teaching as more than a set of texts or ideas that need to be learned. Rather, it is a way of life, a way of seeing the world and responding to the world. It is an ethic of life that provides a distinct angle of vision on all of reality, and is therefore not limited to the explicitly religious topics that are typically the subject of theology classes. If students are to become mature believers who adopt this way of life, this angle of vision, then it needs to be discussed and modeled for them in every classroom.

Of course, this does not mean that science teachers must teach less biology and start teaching theology. It does mean that science teachers should be familiar enough with Catholic social teaching that they can use a lesson in biology or chemistry to reinforce the idea that all of the goods of the earth are gifts from God and human beings are the stewards of those gifts. Teachers in every discipline can find "teachable moments" within their course work to lift up and promote the core values of the Catholic social tradition. Schools might encourage the infusion of Catholic social values in the curriculum by giving special recognition to teachers who "go the extra mile" demonstrating the incorporation of Catholic social teaching in their classrooms.

Consider just a few of the possibilities for integrating Catholic social teaching. Political science readings might provide an opportunity to discuss Catholic teaching on the duty of voting and the role of government in promoting the common good. In economics class, students might use the bishops' pastoral letter on the economy as a lens for analyzing the economy. Government and social studies classes might critique existing tax policies in light of Catholic social principles. Biology students who are studying genetic engineering might be challenged to reflect on the Church's teaching on the sacredness of life. Spanish class might provide an occasion to discuss why Latin American countries have remained so poor and what responsibilities our nation has to the Third World.

CATHOLIC SOCIAL TEACHING IN THE RELIGION CURRICULUM

While responsibility for passing on Catholic social teaching falls on every teacher in every classroom, the religion or theology department plays a fundamental role in teaching students about the Church's social mission in a more formal and structured manner. Theology departments might strive to have at least one required course that provides a basic overview of the Church's social tradition, its history, and its application in the contemporary world.

Specifically, the content of such courses might include a discussion of justice themes in the Bible and a thorough discussion of the key principles of Catholic social teaching as articulated in the papal encyclicals and other Church documents. These courses might explore basic concepts such as justice, the common good, human rights, and the option for the poor. These courses might also include a review of the major movements of Catholic social action during the last 100 years and a discussion of such outstanding historical figures as Pope John XXIII, Dorothy Day, and Archbishop Oscar Romero.

With respect to course readings, it is obvious that many of the encyclical documents are not written in a particularly accessible style. Nonetheless, it is important that students be exposed to at least some of the official texts of the Catholic social tradition. Reading the 1971 Synod document, *Justice in the World*, for example, might provide a rich foundation for discussion and reflection. The major pastoral letters of the U.S. bishops, especially those on peace and economic justice, are also important items to consider. The reading list in Appendix One also provides examples of compendiums in which these documents can be found as well as a source for Pope John Paul II's encyclicals in which the texts are translated into everyday language.

One final point about the content of foundational courses on Catholic social teaching is worth noting. Many students, and adults as well, do not have a clear understanding of the distinction between direct service or "works of charity" and social change or "works of justice." Explaining and exemplifying this distinction should be one of the basic goals of courses devoted to Catholic social thought. Without a clear grasp of this distinction, students are likely to have difficulty understanding the kind of broad social and institutional changes that are called for in Catholic social teaching.

Support from the Administration, Board, and Sponsoring Bodies

Without support from top administration leaders, even the best efforts of teachers may not be as successful as they could be. Clear lines of communication need to be established and fostered between administration, faculty, and staff regarding the role of Catholic social teaching in the school, and the steps that may need to be taken to improve the integration of Catholic social values into every dimension of the institution.

Administration and board members may need to plan special events or programs to assist them in becoming more familiar with the substance of Catholic social teaching and the theological rationale for its central place in Catholic education. Without this understanding, it will be very difficult for them to support the kind of concrete strategies and initiatives that may need to be taken if the Church's social teaching is to become fully integrated into the school's structures, programs, and daily life. A more complete understanding of Catholic social principles may also be beneficial for administrators and board members in that these principles can serve as useful criteria for evaluating how they craft policies, develop procedures, and make decisions related to the school's internal operation.

Mission Statement, Admissions, and Orientation

If a Catholic school's mission statement is an accurate reflection of its guiding philosophy, then its content and language ought to reflect the Church's social mission and the basic principles of Catholic social teaching. Including an explicit reference to Catholic social values in the mission statement strengthens the Catholic identity of the statement and therefore makes it a better instrument for guiding the school's direction.

Likewise, including this element in the mission statement serves a very practical purpose. It communicates to the faculty and staff that this is an important part of the school's life and that they will be supported in their efforts to form students by the values of the Catholic social tradition. It also communicates a similar message to the students, parents, and the public. It says to all who read the mission statement, "We are proud of our Catholic identity. We are proud of our rich tradition of social teaching. We are serious about promoting a more just society and about graduating students who see this as part of their faith and direct their lives toward this goal."

Schools whose current mission statement does not include references to the Church's social mission have a rich opportunity to begin a process of discussion, education, and revision of the mission statement. This can be a teachable moment for faculty, students, parents, board members, and donors.

If Catholic social values are an integral part of a Catholic school, then this should be evident in the admissions and orientation process of the school. Prospective students and parents who inquire about attending the school should see and hear the message that this is a school that embraces the Church's social tradition and teaches its students to live by the values of this tradition.

Consider the situation in which a school was committed to teaching Catholic social values, but did not include this dimension of the school's life in its mission statement and or in its admissions and orientation programs. Some parents, especially if they themselves were unfamiliar with Catholic social teaching, might be surprised and confused to find their sons and daughters discussing and acting on social principles that they find challenging or even objectionable.

Schools will be much more successful in integrating the Church's social values if they work to avoid such surprises. Effective admissions and orientation programs will be those which communicate clearly with parents about the school's commitment to social justice and about the kinds of classes and programs that will help students understand and grapple with the challenging vision of Catholic social teaching. School administrators and teachers may want to consider developing educational strategies and programs regarding this teaching that are designed specifically for parents and alumni/ae. School newsletter articles, adult education events, and invitations to parents to participate in service activities are among some of the varied possibilities.

Finally, school administrators should not overlook the accreditation process as an opportunity to make Catholic social teaching an integral part of the school's life and mission. As a part of the accreditation process, schools can adopt a goal of increasing students' knowledge and application of Catholic social teaching. With this goal established, such vehicles as staff development time, curricular mapping, and program review can be used to infuse the social teaching into the life of the school. Efforts like these can become a very tangible way for a school to express its Catholic identity.

ONGOING SUPPORT MECHANISM FOR TEACHERS

Following initial faculty in-service training, it is important to provide a consistent forum where teachers can share their stories and support one another in their attempts to integrate Catholic social teaching into the classroom. There is no simple blueprint for how this integration is to happen, so teachers need to do much of the translation and implementation on their own.

This makes it especially important that teachers have a chance to meet with other teachers to discuss their experience. What works and what does not work? What values from the Catholic social tradition are most in conflict with contemporary culture and how can teachers handle this tension? What success stories can teachers share with each other regarding the impact of Catholic social teaching on students' lives? What new resources are available to help teachers in this work?

These are the kinds of questions and topics that can be addressed if teachers have a regular opportunity to meet and discuss their experiences. Some of these opportunities can be found within the school itself. For example, teachers and administrators can work to identify a practical means of organizing regular small group discussions on this topic. They might also use faculty newsletters or other established communication means to share ideas and experiences in integrating the social teaching into the classroom.

There is also a real value in sharing ideas with teachers from other schools in the diocese. In one diocese, for example, a project has been created under the name of Catholic Justice Educators' Network (CJEN). This network aims to assist and encourage teachers in their work of justice education. The CJEN network publishes a newsletter in which "bright ideas" or best practices are shared. The network also convenes teachers four times a year to learn about new resources, share each other's stories, and plan joint strategies.

SERVICE AND JUSTICE EXPERIENCES

Most Catholic schools have implemented some form of service learning program in which students are directly involved in activities that serve the poor and benefit the wider community. These programs are popular throughout the country and there exists a wide variety of resource material to assist in organizing these programs.

As valuable and important as these programs are, they often do not include a process for students to reflect on their service experience in the light of Catholic social teaching. This is a serious failing and a missed opportunity since service experiences can and should be linked to a process of social analysis and theological reflection in which the students think more systematically about what they saw, heard, and did in their service project. This kind of analysis and reflection leads students to a deeper understanding of the structures and values that shape the society around them.

For example, students who work at a food pantry or a homeless shelter will learn much more from the experience if they are given the opportunity to think more analytically about the experience and to reflect on it in light of Catholic social teaching. They might begin to ask why all these people are forced to rely on emergency services for food and shelter? Why are they poor? What policies and structures keep them poor? What rights and responsibilities do they have? What does Catholic social teaching tell us about our responsibilities toward the poor? Do the needs of the poor place some moral limits on the rights of the wealthy to accumulate goods? What can we do to work for social changes that will address the deep structural causes of homelessness and hunger?

Integrating Catholic social teaching more deeply with service projects requires intentional discussions during the preparation phase before the service even takes place. It also requires a reflection period after the service activity so that teachers can assist the students in developing critical thinking and social analysis skills. In such settings, students can be taught the value of using Catholic social teaching as a lens through which to view and analyze their experiences with the poor. In addition, teachers would do well to develop opportunities for students to get experience in areas that involve not just works of charity, but also works of justice. Students need to learn not only how to serve food to the hungry; they also need to learn the citizenship skills that will enable them to advocate for social and political changes

> ...students need to learn not only the value of volunteer charity, but also the Christian mandate to work for basic justice and human rights for all.

that would eliminate the root causes of hunger. They need to learn not only what it is like to shelter the homeless, but also what it is like to meet with legislators to request funding for more affordable housing.

In short, students need to learn not only the value of volunteer charity, but also the Christian mandate to work for basic justice and human rights for all. In the words of Pope Pius XI, "Charity will never be true charity unless it takes justice into account ...Let no one attempt with small gifts of charity to exempt himself from the great duties imposed by justice."[33]

INTERNAL POLICIES AND PROCEDURES

The day-to-day decisions, practices, and behaviors within a Catholic school speak volumes about the school's commitment to Catholic social teaching principles. The Synod of Bishops in 1971 expressed the importance of this point when they said: "While the Church is bound to give witness to justice, she recognizes that anyone who ventures to speak to people about justice must first be just in their eyes."[34] Likewise, in the U.S. bishops' pastoral letter on Catholic social teaching and economic justice, they wrote, "All the moral principles that govern the just operation of any economic endeavor apply to the Church and its agencies and institutions; indeed the Church should be exemplary."[35]

Among the internal practices and policies that might be examined in the light of the principles of Catholic social teaching are wages and benefits, due process policies, disciplinary procedures, and investment and purchasing practices. Does the school's budget reflect a commitment to just wages? Does the school provide adequate scholarships for low-income students? Does the school's culture and atmosphere reflect a commitment to peaceful methods of conflict resolution? Do the admissions policies and financial aid practices help to cultivate a student body that is racially and economically diverse?

School administrators and faculty will be able to identify other areas that provide opportunities to put the principles of social justice into practice within the school. Several dioceses, for example, have adopted policies aimed at making sure that school uniforms are not purchased from producers involved with sweatshop labor and the violation of workers' rights.

Such efforts to implement the principles of social justice internally are commendable in themselves, and they make the schools better educational institutions. Equally important is the fact that these actions also send a powerful and positive message to the students about the importance of practicing social justice close to home, in everyday life and in the concrete settings where people work and live.

PRAYER AND WORSHIP LIFE

The Catholic tradition emphasizes the value of communal prayer and outreach to the world. These dimensions of Catholic life are closely linked and mutually reinforcing. An important element in a school's effort to form students in the values of Catholic social thought, therefore, is to provide high-quality liturgical celebrations. These liturgical experiences should expose students to the breadth of prayer traditions within the Church and should consistently demonstrate the important link between liturgy and social justice.

Rev. Virgil Michel, the great liturgical reformer from St. John's University, was well ahead of his time in promoting the public and social dimensions of liturgy. His vision was described in the following way:

> *Michel and his followers spoke of the liturgy as a school of social justice...In the liturgy, properly celebrated, divisions along lines of sex, age, race, or wealth are overcome. In the liturgy, properly celebrated, we learn the ceremonies of respect both for one another... In the celebration of the sacraments, the tendency toward individual self-interest and toward excluding large parts of human experience from what we call the "life of grace" must be constantly overcome. There is no such thing as "spiritual life" or "life in Christ" apart from the relationships that make up human life in the communities in which we live and serve.*[36]

The type of spirituality promoted by prayer and liturgy should have a public as well as a private dimension. Far too often, young Catholic people are being formed by a privatized spirituality that prevents them from connecting their spiritual lives with their public lives. This privatized spirituality is confined to the sphere of intimacy — self, family, friends, and neighbors. It does not extend to the larger sphere beyond the personal and private. It does not relate to the public and institutional structures of culture, politics, and economics.

If liturgy is to be imbued with a commitment to social justice, as Michel suggested it must be, then it needs to nurture a spirituality that is not only private and personal but also public and institutional. It should help students see that the search for salvation takes place not only in the confines of private prayer and individual relationships but also in the public arena of social, economic, and political institutions.

CO-CURRICULAR ACTIVITIES

Life at a Catholic school obviously encompasses more than just classroom activities. After-school activities such as theater, athletics, student government, and school dances are aspects of the school's identity that should not be overlooked. How do these activities reflect or conflict with the values of Catholic social teaching? Are there ways in which they could be enriched by explicit inclusion of Catholic social values and themes? For example, might the choice of theater productions be influenced by the Catholic social tradition? A conscious effort might be made to produce plays that teach a message about human dignity, the quest for justice, and the everyday challenges of people facing unjust systems. Could the mission and agenda of the student government be enhanced by the infusion of Catholic social teaching? Are there opportunities for academic clubs to integrate Catholic social teaching into their activities? Could the parent/student handbook or planner include a page listing and summarizing the major principles from Catholic social teaching?

The ten elements listed above cover many dimensions of daily life in a Catholic school. While the list is not all-inclusive, its scope is intended to emphasize the idea of infusion. As a school's life, mission, faculty, students, and daily activities become more infused with the values and virtues of Catholic social teaching, it becomes more authentically Catholic in its identity. It becomes a sacrament, a sign to the rest of the world, that this is an institution dedicated to helping bring about the reign of God in history. This is a school that believes and acts on the Church's social mission.

Chapter 5

Steps for a Successful Planning Process

We seek to encourage a more integral sharing of the substance of Catholic social teaching in Catholic education and catechesis at every level. The commitment to human life and dignity, to human rights and solidarity, is a calling all Catholic educators must share with their students.

— National Conference of Catholic Bishops[37]

I n order for Catholic schools to be effective in bringing the values of Catholic social teaching into every aspect of the institution, they need to establish a focused and effective planning process to make this happen. Such a process should be directed toward the goal of getting key individuals from every part of the institution involved so that a shared vision can be adopted and coordinated strategies for implementation can be initiated.

This chapter outlines a number of the key steps that faculty and administrators might take as they initiate a planning process. While the initial steps might be accomplished over a period of weeks or months, it is important to adopt a longer-term time frame for the process as a whole. If Catholic social teaching is to be institutionalized and integrated in a comprehensive way, then some of the key elements — such as faculty development and the infusion of social teaching into all academic courses — will require plans and strategies that span years, not weeks or months.

It is also advisable, wherever possible, to incorporate this set of goals and plans into a wider institutional planning process that the school may already have in place. If, for example, there is an established process of planning and implementation for school accreditation, the goal of integrating Catholic social teaching could become a key element of that process.

Whatever process is chosen, the most important step is to begin. Selecting some realistic action steps that are appropriate for the specific school's setting is a good way to get the process started. The following suggestions outline some key elements that may help to identify the best place to begin.

I. Form a Leadership Team

Work with the administration or key faculty members to form a leadership team that will coordinate the overall planning. A good team would be one that is broadly representative of the different dimensions of school life and draws on a diverse mix of faculty, staff members, and students. It is not necessary that team members be specialists or experts in Catholic social teaching or theology. Rather, seek to recruit members who have the interest and energy to work on this initiative and who have the practical knowledge of how to get things done in a school-wide context.

2. Read and Discuss the U.S. Bishops' Statement

Members of the leadership team would do well to begin by reading and studying the bishops' statement, *Sharing Catholic Social Teaching: Challenges and Directions*. This statement provides a clear assessment of the need and the challenges that face Catholic educators in the area of the Church's social teaching. In particular, it explains why Catholic social teaching is absolutely essential to Catholic identity. As the bishops say, teaching the values of Catholic social thought "is not a vocation for a few religion teachers, but a challenge for every Catholic educator...."[38]

> ...teaching the values of Catholic social thought "is not a vocation for a few religion teachers, but a challenge for every Catholic educator."

The bishops' statement is also a useful tool for helping the leadership team to clarify its goals and vision. The statement suggests a broad statement of purpose, but it also identifies important practical elements that need to be addressed, such as faculty formation and integrating social justice with service projects.

3. CONDUCT AN INITIAL ASSESSMENT

With the bishops' statement providing the background and rationale, the leadership team can conduct an initial assessment of the school. This should be a preliminary and informal assessment that helps the team shape a consensus about the goals and tasks that it hopes to pursue. For example, team members might share with each other their own responses to the following questions:

- What are the school's strengths in integrating Catholic social teaching? How does the school currently infuse the Church's social values into the curriculum? How do students currently live out the core values of Catholic social teaching?
- What needs improvement? Where are there gaps? What could be done better?
- What are some of the concrete strategies that the leadership team could adopt in order to address these needs?
- Who are the key people that need to be involved in order to achieve success in implementing these strategies?

4. Meet with Individual Faculty/Staff

The success of the planning process will depend heavily on the degree to which the school's faculty, staff, and administration understand the overall goals and see it in their interest to actively participate in developing and implementing specific strategies aimed at integrating Catholic social teaching throughout the school's structures and programs. In practical terms, this means that the leadership team needs to build support for its efforts by initiating individual conversations with a significant number of faculty and staff members. While there may be a strong temptation to skip over this step and simply announce the leadership team's intentions or persuade others in a collective way that the team's goals are valuable and should be adopted, this would be a mistake for several reasons.

First, it is likely that many faculty members will view Catholic social teaching as being the responsibility of the religion or campus ministry staff. It may not be immediately obvious to them that their own teaching in areas such as math or literature could be enhanced by the infusion of Catholic social values. Individual conversations with these faculty members are a key step, therefore, because they provide an opportunity to explain the overall goal of integrating the Church's social teaching throughout the institution. These conversations can also help faculty members understand why it is important to strengthen the school's Catholic identity, why Catholic social teaching is a key part of that identity, and why every subject and activity in the school can be enriched by infusing the social values of the Church's teaching. Faculty members who are not well trained in theology can also be reassured that the necessary faculty formation and in-service training will be provided to help them be comfortable and competent in discussing Catholic social values in the context of their teaching.

Second, a successful planning process requires that as many people as possible have a sense of ownership for the process and the strategies for implementation that are adopted. By taking several months to meet individually with faculty members and staff, the leadership team can solicit input and advice that will shape the specific strategies that make up a more comprehensive plan. Providing a wide range of people with a chance to participate in shaping the details of the plan will greatly increase their motivation for supporting the final product and for working hard on its implementation.

5. Communicate with Administrators, Board Members, Parents

Throughout the planning process, it is important for the leadership team to communicate regularly with administrators, board members, and parents. The aim should be to position the planning process on Catholic social teaching within the mainstream of the school's activities and decision-making. It should be perceived as an inherent part of the school's ongoing development and growth. Therefore, the leadership team should make a conscious effort to make sure that none of the school's key stakeholders are surprised or uninformed about the initiatives to improve the integration of Catholic social teaching. Regular conversations with the principal and president, ongoing communication with parents, and reports to the school board are possible elements of this strategy.

6. Develop a Comprehensive Plan

This step is the heart of the planning process. It involves discussing and putting on paper a set of specific objectives, strategies, and outcomes that together will achieve the overall goal of integrating Catholic social teaching into all dimensions of the school's life. Each leadership team will have its own preferred way of developing such a plan, but all should strive for plans that are clear, specific, and comprehensive in scope.

When it comes to written planning documents, clarity is a virtue. The objectives, strategies, and intended outcomes should be as concise and as concrete as possible. The writers should try to avoid excessive verbiage and abstract language wherever possible. The strategies and outcomes should be specific in terms of who is going to be responsible for them, the intended timeline or deadline, and any resources that will be necessary for successful implementation. Finally, the plan should be comprehensive in the sense that it cov-

ers the full range of the school's activities and programs. While,
some strategies, like faculty education and formation, may take pre-
cedence in that they logically need to be addressed first, it is important that the overall plan include the full scope of strategies that are
necessary to put Catholic social teaching at the heart of the school's
identity and life. This may mean that the full plan will incorporate a
timeline that extends several years into the future. The key is to
have a single plan that describes all of the strategies and relates
each of them to the central, overarching goal.

7. Implement the Plan

Once the initial plan is developed, the real work of implementation begins. Here the leadership team will want to concentrate on
its role as coordinator and organizer. A successful leadership team
will not do all of the work. The team's members will recruit as many
others as possible to work on individual strategies or tasks that are
part of the overall plan. Typically, these efforts will be organized
into distinct working groups, subcommittees, or task forces. The
leadership team's role is to help form these working groups, encourage them, help them get the necessary resources to carry out
their task, and make sure that their efforts are well coordinated with
the other initiatives that are being undertaken.

The leadership team plays a key role in ensuring that the agreed-
upon plans and strategies actually get implemented. While the team
members need not do all the work, they should strive to hold themselves and others accountable for carrying out the tasks that they
agreed to perform. Sometimes a polite but firm reminder might be
necessary to revive specific initiatives if key people drop the ball or
get sidetracked with other priorities. Maintaining this kind of ac-
countability sends a signal to everyone about the seriousness of the
planning process and the valuable benefits that it will produce for
the whole school.

8. Evaluate and Celebrate

It has been said that if something is worth doing, it is worth
evaluating. This certainly holds true for the process of integrating

Catholic social values into the programs and practices of Catholic schools. If the school administrators and leadership team are to avoid the danger of Catholic social teaching being treated as a passing fad or a designated theme for the year, then the planning process requires a long term commitment and a willingness to make adjustments along the way. Ongoing evaluation can help make that happen.

Throughout the implementation phase of the planning process, it is important to evaluate the progress that is being made, to discuss unforeseen obstacles that may have arisen, and to modify the specific objectives and strategies as needed. The leadership team should discuss and adopt evaluation methodologies that are ongoing and that fit the particular circumstances of their leadership team and their school.

In constructing specific categories or questions for various evaluation tools, the team may want to use the essential elements listed in Chapter Four as a framework to ensure that the planning process incorporates all dimensions of the school's life.

Finally, the leadership team should make a conscious effort to publicly recognize and celebrate the progress that is being made as the implementation process proceeds. Whether they are small-scale recognitions of individual successes and innovations or larger scale celebrations of school-wide achievements, these efforts will provide the kind of positive reinforcement and encouragement that build everyone's confidence and enthusiasm for continuing their good work.

Chapter 6

Virtues and Skills
of Catholic School Graduates

What would the ideal Catholic school student look like? What habits of thought and action would such a student have acquired by the time of graduation? Focusing on these questions is one good way to develop a shared vision for integrating Catholic social teaching into one's school. This approach emphasizes outcomes. It asks faculty and staff to imagine the characteristics and habits of the ideal Catholic school graduate. Being clear about these desired outcomes can help educators in developing specific concrete strategies to achieve these outcomes.

What, then, might be some of the personal and social characteristics of graduates who had learned and assimilated the core values of Catholic social teaching? Every teacher and faculty member may have a unique list of virtues and skills, but I offer the following as a starting point for discussion.

A Social Faith

Catholic students who are true to the Church's teaching practice a faith that is not only private, but also social. Their prayer life and spirituality as well as their participation in the sacraments have a private and personal dimension, but they also incorporate a social and communal aspect. For example, Catholic students understand sin and grace as having important social meaning. They are committed to working against the structures of sin, such as institutional racism and extreme economic inequality. They also see God's grace in the social dimensions of everyday life. In the words of St. Ignatius of Loyola, they are able to "see God in all things." These students see themselves as having a mission in the world. They are committed to having a career but they also see it as a vocation. They know how to bring their faith into every dimension of their life.

Respect

Respect for human dignity is an anchor for the Catholic vision of social justice. Catholic students who successfully adopt this vision have a basic respect for other human beings. They believe that all people are made in God's image and that human life is therefore sacred. They judge the worth of others in terms of who they are as human beings, not what they have materially, how much power they wield, or what color their skin is.

> They believe that all people are made in God's image and that human life is therefore sacred. They judge the worth of others in terms of who they are as human beings, not what they have materially, how much power they wield, or what color their skin is.

Their respect for the dignity of others leads them to have a deep commitment to justice in their individual dealings with others. They are recognized as persons of integrity and fairness. They also understand that respect and justice must go beyond private, individual relationships. They require that social, economic, and political structures be organized in such a way that they promote human dignity and protect the basic human rights that are necessary for human beings to flourish.

SOCIAL RESPONSIBILITY

Catholic students know and understand that all human beings are social by nature. They realize that interdependence, their inter-relatedness with others, is natural and good. They understand the concept of the common good, and they are committed to working cooperatively with others to build up and maintain the common good. They have the practical skills to work in groups, to negotiate, to find common ground, and to reach an agreement on common goals and strategies.

COMPASSION FOR AND WITH THE POOR

The Latin roots of the word "compassion" mean to "suffer with." Thus, compassion is the virtue that enables one to feel passionately for and with others. Catholic students who practice this virtue are able to go beyond their private interests and reach out to be in solidarity with those in need.

They act on their compassion by performing works of both charity and justice. Through works of charity, they put themselves regularly in contact with the poor and the needy. They not only provide direct service for them, but also get to know them and understand them. At the same time, these Catholic students know that charity is not enough. They are committed to work for justice by changing the social and economic structures and institutions that are the root causes of suffering and injustice.

SOLIDARITY

Catholic students are global citizens. They understand their moral responsibilities to others around the globe. They know that they are networked not only technologically and economically, but also in profoundly religious and moral ways with all other human beings. Therefore, these students make conscious choices in their everyday lives that reflect their solidarity with the poor of the world. They examine their purchasing and consuming habits in order to find ways in which they can support economic justice around the world.

These Catholic students are also adept at looking at the world and its issues from other points of view besides their own. For example, they are open to a more global perspective on issues of peace and to Third World perspectives on questions of economic policy. They are able to see the world from the perspective of the economically poor and the politically weak.

STEWARDSHIP

Catholic students know that all of creation is a gift, and they demonstrate a sense of awe and reverence in the face of this gift. They know that the goods of the earth, including their own private possessions, are not ultimately theirs to use as they see fit. They realize that they are stewards and that they hold the goods of the earth in trust. Therefore, they have a profound respect for natural resources, and they work hard to be environmentally responsible in their daily consumption habits.

These Catholic students do not put excessive importance on consumer goods, and they do not equate happiness with the accumulation of material things. As a result, they consciously strive to lead lives of relative simplicity, to keep their lives from becoming cluttered with unnecessary material goods. They are not afraid to stand apart from the consumerism and materialism of American culture because they know that people are more important than things and being is more important than having.

WORK

These graduates have a Catholic work ethic. That is to say, they see all work as having dignity because work is an activity of the human person. They understand that work is, in a very real sense, a religious activity. It is carrying on God's work that was begun with creation. When these Catholic students engage in work, whether it is academic work or any form of employment, they approach it with an understanding of the spiritual and faith dimensions. In their choice of careers, these students are careful to look for jobs in which they can make a lasting commitment to the common good. They see their future work life as a vocation, and they will often sacrifice clear financial rewards for the sake of jobs or careers that are more meaningful in social and spiritual terms.

SOCIAL ANALYSIS

Catholic graduates have a demonstrated ability to conduct social analysis. They have a deep-seated commitment to truth, and they have developed a critical consciousness. They know how to analyze social trends and institutions. These students keep up with current events. They read daily newspapers, journals, and books of social commentary. They know how to interpret the signs of the times and to engage in critical reflection about the information and events that are before them.

These students are not afraid to be counter-cultural when the values of their faith demand it. They are confident about the personal, social, and religious values that they believe in, and they feel comfortable in offering a critique of the culture around them. They also have the courage to act on their beliefs, even when it may be unpopular or may bring them into conflict with others.

CITIZENSHIP SKILLS

Catholic graduates are active and skilled citizens. They believe in politics as a positive instrument for achieving the common good, and they are committed to making it work. They are committed to being knowledgeable voters who follow the major issues, learn about the candidates and issues, and go to the polls. They know how to use the values of Catholic teaching to analyze the candidates, and they judge the candidates based on a wide spectrum of issues.

These students also have practical political skills. They know how to write a good letter to their legislator, how to plan and conduct a group visit with a politician, and how to write a good letter to the editor on a political issue. They also know how to get involved in the campaigns of candidates. They have experience in knocking on doors and passing out leaflets for candidates, in helping with get-out-the-vote campaigns, and in participating in political conventions.

ORGANIZING SKILLS

Catholic students are competent leaders. They see themselves as "history makers" and they have both the desire and the skills to effect change in society. This means that at a practical level these students have concrete organizing skills. They know how to build relationships with others, how to recruit allies, how to plan an agenda, run a good meeting, research an issue, raise money, and deal with the media. They can analyze and use power effectively and they know how to develop a winnable strategy for success. They know how to deal creatively and positively with tension, and they are not afraid of conflict and controversy. They are passionate about their values and goals, but pragmatic and competent when it comes to getting results.

PEACE

A final characteristic of Catholic graduates is that they are people of peace. Due to their deep respect for the sacred dignity of all persons, they understand that doing violence to others is a form of doing violence to God. Therefore, they are committed to practicing the virtue of peace in a positive, proactive way. They always strive to find peaceful means of resolving differences and they are skilled in mediation — assisting others in reconciling their differences and finding common ground. These students are also people of peace in terms of their social and political view regarding national and international relations. They are knowledgeable about the history of nonviolence and are committed to using it as an instrument for achieving justice.

The virtues listed above are among the qualities that one might hope to see in a Catholic school graduate. To the extent that graduates embody these characteristics, their teachers and mentors can take pride in having nurtured and sent forth faith-filled Catholics who will be leaders and disciples. They will be a leaven in the modern world.

In closing this chapter, I share with you an e-mail message addressed to this year's graduating class. I believe it captures much of the spirit of mission and discipleship that is at the heart of Catholic social teaching.

Email to graduates@class.of.2000

Dear Grads,

As you embark on your journey into the future, I thought you might appreciate a few words of wisdom, a few tools or principles to use along way. Here is my simple little offering — a three-part formula for living life with meaning.

1. Observe — The ability to see reality clearly is one of the foundations for sound decision making. It will help you to lead a good life. Learn to develop a keen sense of observation. Try to see actively, not passively. Look beneath the surface for that which is most important.

Go out of your way to put yourself in new situations in order to observe more of the world and to see it more directly. Do not simply rely on the media, hearsay, or on popular myths as the basis for your thinking. See for yourself.

Observe all aspects of your world, not just the familiar, the easy, and the near at hand. See the rich and the poor, the far and the near, that which is like you and that which is different. See with an inquiring mind, an open heart, and a compassionate soul. Always see with a vision that knows that all of creation is a gift from God.

2. Judge — This is perhaps the most important step. Judging in this sense means making sound judgments based on values. It means stepping back to do reflection and analysis in order to bring your deepest values to bear on the reality you have seen. It means getting beneath the surface and asking the "why" questions. Why are some people rich and some poor? Why, in such a prosperous land, do so many thousands line up each day at soup kitchens and homeless shelters? Why do so many families break up? Why is violence so prevalent?

This process takes time. It requires a conscious effort because, in our fast paced world, it is easy to skip over this step and to go directly from seeing to acting. To do so is to forego the thoughtful reflection that can provide meaning and integrity in our lives. It is to act without making conscious moral choices. In short, it is to react rather than to act.

Making sound moral judgments cannot be done in a vacuum. You need tools, guidelines, and principles that constitute a source of wisdom to draw upon in times of difficult choices. Let me suggest two from our Catholic tradition.

The Bible is one source. Get to know it. Think of it not as a blueprint for action, but as a collection of wisdom. It is a book that can help us sort out what is important and what is not. It contains a rich treasure of guidelines and criteria about how to know oneself, how to treat others, and how to relate to all of creation.

A second source of wisdom that can guide your reflection is Catholic social teaching, a body of teaching that can change your life. This teaching says that people are more important than things and that being is more important than having. It says that we are all social beings — not isolated individuals but members of one family. This teaching tells us that a basic requirement for leading a meaningful life and for shaping a healthy community is that we all give special attention to the needs of the poor. This is a form of wisdom which says that we will ultimately be judged by how we treat the poorest and most powerless members of our community.

3. Act — If you have seen clearly and reflected deeply in order to make sound moral judgments, then you will know what is right. But knowing and saying what is right is not the same as doing what is right. Ultimately, you will be judged by your actions — both what you do and what you fail to do. Sometimes acting justly requires courage, trust, and the willingness to take risks. As difficult as that may sometimes seem, know that the rewards are very real.

Observe. Judge. Act. It is a process that has stood the test of time. I hope it works for you.

Chapter 7

Samples and Examples

This chapter includes a series of concrete examples of how the values of Catholic social teaching can be integrated into the various dimensions of a school's life. These examples range from faculty training and formation initiatives to special projects within the existing curriculum. They include a sampling of ideas not only from religion and social studies classes, where the connection to social justice concerns may be more obvious, but also from other subjects such as computer technology and math, where Catholic social values can be incorporated in more indirect ways.

This sampling of ideas, resources, and concrete initiatives is offered as a way of demonstrating the wide range of strategies that can be adopted if one takes seriously the goal of integrating Catholic social teaching into the educational experience of Catholic schools. These items are not necessarily the best or the ideal models for each category that is covered. Rather, they are simply examples of what

This sampling of ideas, resources, and concrete initiatives is offered as a way of demonstrating the wide range of strategies that can be adopted if one takes seriously the goal of integrating Catholic social teaching into the educational experience of Catholic schools.

some teachers have done to help students understand and act on the values of Catholic social teaching.

Faculty Development

A "workshop on wheels" was the first step in a long-term plan adopted by Hill-Murray Catholic High School in Maplewood, MN as a means to help the school's staff understand and implement Catholic social teaching. The school's administrators asked the teachers and staff to go on an all-day bus tour as part of their back-to-school preparations for the start of the new school year. The bus tour itself was a means of helping teachers and staff to see firsthand the realities of poverty and wealth in their metropolitan region. They visited very poor inner city neighborhoods, neighborhoods that were in transition, and very wealthy developments on the outer fringes of the metropolitan region.

The trip was more than just a tour, however. It was set in the context of prayer and reflection on Catholic social teaching. Along the way, participants were also given printed resources and a running commentary by the staff from the diocesan social justice office regarding the social, economic, and political factors that influence why some neighborhoods are desperately poor and other are extremely rich. This analysis helped to lift up the social justice issues that lay behind the realities that the teachers and staff members saw from inside the bus.

This bus tour was the launching pad for a long-term strategy that the school adopted for faculty development on Catholic social teaching. Through the year, they scheduled a series of in-service speakers on Catholic social teaching, its biblical roots, and its implications for contemporary social issues. Faculty members also participated in small group study and reflection on these topics, and individual departments met with specialists who provided materials to help them develop plans for integrating Catholic social teaching into all aspects of the curriculum. They also made plans for sending several faculty members each summer to a week-long course on Catholic social teaching in order to get a deeper understanding of the roots of this teaching.

As a means of anchoring these faculty development activities in the life of the school, the administration incorporated them into the planning that is part of the school's accreditation process. They also printed a list of major principles from Catholic social teaching in the school's student/parent handbook. To bring parents onboard, the assistant principal prepared an extensive lead article for the school newsletter. Under the title of "Faculty Explore Church's 'Best Kept Secret,'" the article explained why the faculty was engaging in this ambitious development program and why it was important to the Catholic identity of the school.

This example reflects a thorough and long-term approach to faculty development. It is the kind of approach that can serve to lay a solid foundation for integrating social teaching into all dimensions of the school's life.

CROSS-CURRICULUM PROJECT

Linda Hanson was a technology teacher when she discovered the riches of Catholic social teaching. In an effort to make the social teaching principles concrete and real for her students, she developed the "Poverty Project." Although originally designed for junior high school students, this teaching module can easily be adapted for other grade levels.

The "Poverty Project" began with a simple question: "How many people in this room have broken a leg?" Two of students raised their hands. When asked, 'How could the rest of us, who have not broken a leg, understand what it feels like?" They came up with several responses. "We could ask a person who had broken their leg what it is like...We could use crutches for a day."

This exchange began a five-month long journey in which these young students discovered what it feels like to be poor — without being poor. The twenty activities encompassing this cross-curriculum unit are called the "Poverty Project."

Since simulation, not lecture, is critical in bringing the reality of poverty to teenagers, every activity introduced during the "Poverty Project" was geared towards student-based, hands-on learning. Their journey began when the students conducted a role playing exercise, taking on the role of a single parent with two children, ages seven and two. They developed a budget based on a desired lifestyle for their family. They chose an apartment in the classified ads, chose a car they wanted to lease, chose public or private education for their children, evaluated and priced daycare for their toddler. One of the students even named her two children. The total of their expenses equaled the salary they needed to earn to support their desired lifestyle. Then it was back to the classifieds to discover four jobs that would support their budgeted expenses.

One morning they were handed a pink slip. Through no fault of their own, they had been laid off. They had no extended family to help, and no prospect of finding a job. After researching both the current minimum wage and the current welfare allotment for a family of three in their state, they had to make a choice between going on welfare or accepting a minimum wage job. They were asked if they felt any differently personally, not financially, when they were earning a minimum wage versus accepting welfare allotments.

Now they had to go back to the drawing board! The students had to scale back their desired budget. They went from leasing a car to calling the bus company for the price of a monthly bus pass. They discovered that Food Stamps really help stretch options. Using grocery store advertisements, they bought food for their family for a month within the constraints of their allocation.

The worst was yet to come. One morning they received eviction notices. They had five minutes to get everything out of their lockers that they would need for the day — books, assignments, coats, lunches, gym bags, etc. The only time they could set their belongings down was when they were seated. If they failed to follow this rule, their possessions would be confiscated. Reflecting on this experience, one girl wrote that she was so frustrated she could have screamed. Another student said she would look at homeless people so differently — she now understood how exhausting life could be.

Then the real work began. Working in small groups, the students chose a subtopic of poverty and produced a computerized slide show with an accompanying script. They uncovered that the average age of a homeless person in America is nine and that a livable wage is $10.73, almost double the current minimum wage. They learned how to make phone calls to dig for information, even when adults were rude to them. They learned the difference between charity and social justice and how we, as Christians, have not an option, but an obligation, to carry out both works.

These students also learned that they have the power to make a difference in this world by staying informed and communicating their knowledge. They learned that their research was worthy of being published on the Internet and presented to 200 people at the culmination of the "Poverty Project" at a school-wide "Hunger Banquet." The daily newspaper even covered this event.

The students concluded the "Poverty Project" with the following prayer:

On the street I saw a small girl cold and shivering in a thin dress, with little hope of a decent meal. I became angry and said to God: "Why did you permit this? Why don't you do something about it?"

For a while God said nothing. That night God replied quite suddenly: "I certainly did something about it. I made you."

The "Poverty Project" has been published by Common Ground Press (1-800-232-5533) as a ready-to-use social justice course of 20 sessions, plus 20 additional sessions, for young people to research, write, and create infomercials about poverty. The materials teach research and communication skills and can involve social studies, religion, literature, and technology studies. Detailed lesson plans and dozens of reproducible handouts are included.

SOCIAL STUDIES / SOCIAL JUSTICE

Kevin LaNave, a teacher at Cathedral High School in St. Cloud, MN, has a social justice activity he calls "Speed Monopoly." This is an exercise that may be done in one class meeting or across several. Here are the steps:

1. Prepare a Monopoly game for five players. Set up envelopes in this manner:
   • One envelope that contains almost all of the properties (including some monopolies) and significant amounts of money.
   • Two envelopes that contain a couple of pieces of property and some money ($200-$300).
   • Two envelopes that contain a small amount of money ($100-$200) and no property
2. Players begin taking turns, and all standard Monopoly rules are followed — except that when someone goes bankrupt, he or she is allowed to borrow money from the bank with the understanding that the money will be repaid once he or she has earned more. Keep track of amounts owed.
3. Usually within a few turns, those without property will become bankrupt. Middle-income players will likely follow suit. The wealthiest will typically increase their wealth. Once the following trends are becoming evident, stop the game.

Mr. LaNave has an excellent description of how to do a group processing of the effects of "Speed Monopoly." It is available on pages 73-76 of the teacher's edition textbook entitled *Christian Justice* published by St. Mary's Press (1-800-533-8095).

In addition to using "Speed Monopoly" and other techniques in class, Mr. LaNave also gives his students some concrete lessons in political advocacy. He brings a busload of students to a legislative lobbying event called "Day on the Hill." This is an annual event sponsored by a statewide ecumenical lobbying organization. He uses the one and a half hour bus ride to St. Paul to brief the students and prepare them for the event.

In the morning, they attend briefing sessions on specific legislative issues affecting the poor and participate in skills workshops on how to lobby their legislators. In the afternoon, they visit with their legislators and put their advocacy skills into practice. The day concludes with a large rally in the rotunda of the state capital. As part of the follow-up reflection and debriefing, Mr. LaNave helps the students connect the principles of Catholic social teaching to the information they have learned and the experiences they have had.

MATH

At first glance, it might seem that math teachers would have a hard time trying to integrate Catholic social thought into their teaching. A closer look, however, reveals that there are some interesting possibilities, especially in terms the kinds of real life examples that one uses to demonstrate or test mathematical knowledge.

One excellent resource for math teachers is a booklet entitled "Math for a Change," published by the Mathematics Teachers Association. This is a resource that is written by teachers and intended to "make their students more aware of injustices in the world, and at the same time to make their teaching more interesting and effective." Its contents include descriptions of 38 situations of injustice that need mathematics in order to be fully understood. Here is an example from the booklet:

#17: Race and Poverty Trends in the U.S.A.

In spite of efforts to eliminate income disparity between Whites and African-Americans, gaps still do persist. Consider the following data on poverty in our county.

Number of Poor in Thousand	Percent of Poor
African-Americans — 9,302	30.7%
Whites — 20,784	10.0%
Total Americans — 31,528	12.8%

All information is based on 1989 statistics. At that time, a family of four was poor if its income was $12,674 or less. Please answer the following:

- Notice that the sum of the African-American poor and the poor Whites does not equal the total given on the third line. Why is this so?
- From the data in the table, figure out how many African-Americans there were in 1989. How many White Americans?

- What is wrong with this reasoning? — Since 10% of Whites are poor and 30.7% of African-Americans are poor, the percent of Whites and African-American poor must be the average of 10% and 30.7%—which is 20.35%
- The poor Whites combined with the African-American poor made up what percent of the total number of Americans in 1989?
- Suggest reasons why the poverty rate for African-Americans is more than three times as great as that for Whites.

"Math for a Change" can be ordered for $12.50 per copy by writing to Kevin J. Mistrik, Loyola Academy, 1100 N. Laramie, Wilmette, IL 60091. Please make checks payable to the Mathematics Teachers Association.

RELIGION

At the Academy of the Holy Angels in Richfield, MN, a team of creative high school religion teachers jointly planned an innovative project for the social justice class that is a requirement for all juniors. Each of the ten sections of the junior class began by learning about the Catholic social teaching principles. They discussed how these principles relate to the issues of welfare and poverty, and they began to learn more about the realities of welfare in their city.

Each section of the class invited staff members from the local Catholic Charities to speak with the students about some of the myths and facts about the poor and those who are on welfare. Students then went through the process of trying to plan a family budget based on a welfare grant. They also learned about the application process for welfare and discovered some of the bureaucratic obstacles that low-income families face when applying for assistance. Then, all of the class sections met for a special joint session in which they heard from three women who were actually on welfare. The women shared their stories and answered questions from the students about realities of trying to make ends meet on welfare.

The next step was for students to take a bus tour to see firsthand the realities of poverty in their city. The religion faculty planned this tour with the help of Catholic Charities staff members. However, it became clear that taking more than 150 students on a bus tour was not a workable option. As an alternative, each section of the junior class was asked to choose three representatives to go on the bus tour. These representatives were given the responsibility of going on the tour and then reporting back what they saw and what they learned.

The bus tour included a visit to very low-income neighborhoods and a stop at a homeless shelter where hundreds of men slept on simple mats on the floor every evening. The tour also took the students to changing neighborhoods and included a discussion of the public policies and other social and institutional factors that together produce a development process that concentrates poverty in the core of the city, while middle class and wealthy families are drawn to the outer ring suburbs. Seeing and discussing these kinds of sharp disparities helped the students to understand that poverty is not a completely isolated and distinct reality. Rather, it is part of a wider complex of social and economic policies that influence the rich and poor alike.

Following the bus tour and the debriefing of the experience, the participants returned to their respective class sections and gave a full report to all of the students. This led to further discussions about poverty, wealth, and the social teaching principles that help inform Catholics of their responsibilities to the poor.

This example demonstrates a good mix of experiential learning along with social analysis and critical reflection based on Catholic social teaching. In the end, the students not only learned about the realities of poverty and welfare but also were introduced to some of the Church's social teaching and were challenged to begin thinking about how they can live their lives as believers who are committed to relieving suffering and fighting injustice.

STUDENT GOVERNMENT

The overall mission of a school's student government and the specific activities that its members undertake provide a good opportunity to introduce the values of Catholic social teaching. The following example is from an elementary school, but it could readily serve as a model for student government at the high school level as well.

The students at St. John Vianney School in South St. Paul, MN have a tradition of celebrating Catholic Schools Week at the end of January. Each year they invite community leaders — the mayor, the police chief, and other local representatives — to attend various festivities at the school.

Several years ago, the student council, made up of leaders from 4th through 6th grade, decided that they wanted to focus more attention on social justice issues. After seeking input from teachers and archdiocesan staff, the students decided to write a "Proclamation for Social Justice" that would be presented to the mayor and other public leaders who would be visiting the school.

They proceeded to discuss and draft their proclamation. Then, on the designated day, with the mayor and other public officials in attendance, the chairperson of the student council stood before the guests and read the proclamation.

We, the students at St. John Vianney School, believe that all people regardless of how old they are, where they live, what kind of job they have, the color of their skin, and the amount of education they have all deserve to be treated justly and be given the same opportunities to live good lives. Therefore, we ask you as our government leaders to:

- Keep funding child care for people trying to better themselves and get off welfare.
- Help keep our neighborhoods safe for us and our families.
- Try to provide shelter and meals for all who need it, especially the little children.
- Protect the elderly and poor families from having their heat turned off.
- Increase the minimum wage so that parents can take better care of their children without government help.
- Protect the lives of the unborn and the elderly because they are just as important as the rest of us.

We are trying to do our part here at school, in our neighborhoods, and in our community but we cannot do it alone. Please help us and do what you can to see that all people are treated justly and have an equal chance for a happy, healthy, and safe future for themselves and their families.

Learning the Public Skills of Citizenship

St. Bernard's is a K-12 Catholic school in St. Paul, MN that is home to a program called "Public Achievement." This initiative began almost a decade ago and has spread to more than thirty other schools in Minnesota and elsewhere. It is a unique and successful program that trains and empowers students to be effective agents for change in the public arena.

"Public Achievement" describes itself as "an experience-based civic education program for young people ages 8 to 18." The core of the program centers on organized groups of students who identify issues and design their own action strategies for bringing about change. One of the key elements is that these students are "coached" by college students and other adults, who guide the groups, train the students in specific public skills, and help them reflect on the group's goals and their progress in achieving those goals.

At the beginning of each year, the students of St. Bernard's gather for a large "issue convention" at which issues are proposed and selected and issue groups are recruited. Several years ago, for example, a group was formed around the issue of land mines. Some students had read about the problem and were appalled by what they dis-

> We...believe that all people regardless of how old they are, where they live, what kind of job they have, the color of their skin, and the amount of education they have all deserve to be treated justly and be given the same opportunities to live good lives.

covered. Said one student named Veronica, "I joined the 'Public Achievement' group on land mines because I was sick and tired of hearing about innocent children and adults getting their legs blown off, left with suffering for the rest of their lives. I do not think that God put us on this earth to kill and hurt one another. I think he put us on earth to be united with one another."

The group focusing on the land mines issue was taught by their coaches to ask questions such as: How is the land mine issue connected to social justice and the teachings of Jesus Christ? Who are the stakeholders and how can we influence them? Who has the power to help us and how can we contact them? How are decisions made and how can we affect decisions? Why should others care?

This issue group contacted an international organization working to ban land mines and learned that this organization had a bus touring the country to educate citizens about the issue. The students convinced the organization to bring the bus to their school so that the whole school could get involved. They also joined the "Catholic Campaign to Ban Land Mines," and they organized a letter writing campaign to President Clinton urging support for an international ban.

Students who participate in the many issue groups at St. Bernard's learn very specific skills. With the aid of their coaches, they learn important citizenship skills such as how to research an issue, how to plan an agenda, how to run a good meeting, and how to meet with public officials and other decision makers. They also learn important reflection and analysis skills such as how to evaluate issues and actions in light of Catholic social teaching. Yet, in the end, what is most important about St. Bernard's students is not the specific skills they learn but the fact that they become confident and competent shapers of history.

SCHOOL DISCIPLINE PROGRAM

A school's discipline program can provide a variety of teachable moments. At Hill-Murray Catholic High School in Maplewood, MN, the school administrators begin the school year with class meetings to cover the student handbook. The key principles of Catholic social teaching are included in the handbook, and as they explain the focus for the year, the administrators refer to the social teachings as a context for the specific discipline policies. A conscious effort is made to emphasize the dignity of each student, his or her place within the school community, and the rights and responsibilities each member has. Rules are explained as a way for the school to protect the rights of the each individual and vulnerable members of the community.

Each student is challenged to exercise his or her freedom in a manner that contributes to the good of the community. Restorative justice methods are also used to facilitate conflict among members of the community, among students, and among students and staff members. Respect, collaboration, and covenant are themes explored and agreed upon in resolving differences. Even the principle of subsidiarity finds a place within the system, allowing students the ability to work out their differences without adult intervention and encouraging teachers to develop classroom expectations reflecting the same emphasis on justice.

The examples presented here demonstrate a variety of creative ways that educators can use Catholic social thought to enrich their own teaching and to inspire their students to think and act as agents of God's love and justice. By undertaking such efforts, teachers and faculty make a lasting contribution to the Catholic identity of their schools.

Conclusion

The Church shares the same earthly lot with the world:
it is to be a leaven and, as it were, the soul of human
society in its renewal by Christ and transformation into
the family of God.

— Second Vatican Council[39]

A wise old theology instructor once summed up the Catholic vision of faithful discipleship by saying, "We are supposed to be the leaven in the loaf, not part of the lump!" This is perhaps a useful image to remember when thinking about Catholic social teaching and the key role that it plays in Catholic identity.

Students who graduate from Catholic schools are called go forth with a mission in the world. They are called strive to be a leaven in society. By the way they think and act, by the values they profess, and by the work they do on behalf of human dignity and social justice, these graduates can be a visible sign of the Church's social mission and the social values that undergird that mission.

Educators who help prepare and form these students have both a profound responsibility and a wonderful vocation. May their deepening knowledge of Catholic social teaching be an effective and rewarding means of carrying out this vocation.

Endnotes

1. National Conference of Catholic Bishops, *Sharing Catholic Social Teaching: Challenges and Directions* (Washington, DC: United States Catholic Conference, 1998), p. 3.

2. Ibid., p. 6-7.

3. National Conference of Catholic Bishops, *Communities of Salt and Light* (Washington, DC: United States Catholic Conference, 1993), p. 3.

4. Synod of Bishops, *Justice in the World*, 1971, #6.

5. John R. Donahue, S.J., "Biblical Perspectives on Justice," in John C. Haughey, S.J., ed., *The Faith that Does Justice* (New York: Paulist Press, 1977), p. 109.

6. Ibid.

7. Walter Brueggemann, "Voices of the Night," in Walter Brueggemann, Sharon Parks, Thomas Groome, *To Act Justly, Love Tenderly, Walk Humbly* (Eugene, OR: Wipf & Stock Publishers, 1997), p. 5.

8. Gerhard von Rad, *Old Testament Theology*, trans. D. M. G Stalker (New York: Harper and Bros., 1962), p. 370.

9. Donohue, p. 69.

10. Walter Burghardt, *Preaching the Just Word* (New Haven: Yale Univ. Press, 1998), p. 3.

11. Thomas Groome, *Educating for Life* (Chicago: Thomas More Press, 1998), p. 366.

12. Ibid., p. 367.

13. National Conference of Catholic Bishops, *Economic Justice for All: Catholic Social Teaching and the U.S. Economy* (Washington, DC: United States Catholic Conference, 1986), #38.

14. Groome, p. 367-368.

15. Vatican Council, *Pastoral Constitution on the Church and the Modern World*, 1965, #1.

16. National Conference of Catholic Bishops, *Sharing Catholic Social Teaching*, p. 4.

17. Vatican Council, *Pastoral Constitution*, #76.

18. National Conference of Catholic Bishops, *Economic Justice for All*, #28.

19. Ibid., #80.

20. Pope John Paul II, "Address to Bishops of Brazil," *Origins* (July 31, 1980): 35.

21. National Conference of Catholic Bishops, *Economic Justice for All*, #88.

22. Ibid., #87.

23. Ibid., #77.

24. National Conference of Catholic Bishops, *Sharing Catholic Social Teaching*, p. 5.

25. Vatican Council, *Pastoral Constitution*, #69.

26. National Conference of Catholic Bishops, *Renewing the Earth* (Washington, DC: United States Catholic Conference, 1991), p. 6.

27. National Conference of Catholic Bishops, *Called to Global Solidarity* (Washington, DC: United States Catholic Conference, 1997), #1.

28. Pope John Paul II, *On Social Concern*, 1988, #38.

29. Pope John Paul II, *The Hundredth Year*, 1991, #51.

30. Pope John Paul II, "Homily at Bagington Airport," *Origins* (June 10, 1982): 55.

31. Vatican Council, *Pastoral Constitution*, #78.

32. National Conference of Catholic Bishops, *Sharing Catholic Social Teaching*, p. 2.

33. Pope Pius XI, *Divini Redemptoris*, 1937, #49.

34. Synod of Bishops, *Justice in the World*, 1971, #40.

35. National Conference of Catholic Bishops, *Economic Justice for All*, #347.

36. Msgr. Jack Egan, "Liturgy and Justice: An Unfinished Agenda," *Origins* (September 22, 1983): 251.

37. National Conference of Catholic Bishops, *Sharing Catholic Social Teaching*, p. 6.

38. Ibid.

39. Vatican Council, *Pastoral Constitution*, #40.

Appendix I

Suggested Readings and Resources

(Note: The following list of readings and resources has been compiled by the author and reflects his opinion of each source.)

INTRODUCTORY WORKS

- National Conference of Catholic Bishops, *Sharing Catholic Social Teaching: Challenges and Directions*. Washington, DC: United States Catholic Conference, 1998.

  This statement by the U.S. bishops makes a strong appeal to Catholic educators to integrate the Church's social teaching into all aspects of Catholic education. It includes an assessment of the needs, a summary of the major themes from Catholic social thought, and practical suggestions and recommendations for Catholic educators at all levels.

- Fred Kammer, SJ, *Doing Faith Justice: An Introduction to Catholic Social Thought*. New York: Paulist Press, 1991.

   This is an excellent introduction to Catholic social teaching. Written in a very popular style, this book is both interesting and inspirational. It includes stories, commentaries on the Church's teaching, and brief summaries of many of the official papal encyclicals on social justice.

- Marvin L. Krier Mich, *Catholic Social Teaching and Movements*. Mystic, CT: Twenty-Third Publications, 1998.

   This is a superb introduction to Catholic social teaching. It covers not only the official documents and encyclicals but also describes the movements and people who embodied the struggle for social justice in the last 100 years. It is very well written and makes the Catholic tradition of social justice come alive.

- Thomas Groome, *Educating for Life: A Spiritual Vision for Every Teacher and Parent*. Allen, TX: Thomas More Press, 1998.

   If one is looking for one general essay that summarizes and explains Catholic social teaching, it is hard to beat the eighth chapter of this recent book by Dr. Thomas Groome. This is an exceptional work overall, and the chapter on Catholic social teaching is superb. As the title suggests, it is directed at teachers and parents.

- Peter Henroit, Edward DeBerri, and Michael Schultheis, *Catholic Social Teaching: Our Best Kept Secret*. Maryknoll, NY: Orbis Books, 1988.

   This handy little work begins with a brief overview of the development of social teaching. The core of the book consists of detailed outlines of the major social teaching documents from 1891 to 1988. It is a very convenient reference to have.

- *Momentum*. Washington, DC: NCEA, August/September, 1997. (The journal of the National Catholic Educational Association)

   This issue of Momentum is devoted to the theme of Catholic social teaching and education. It includes over twenty articles on specific themes from the teaching to how these themes can be applied in educational settings.

- *The Busy Christian's Guide to Catholic Social Teaching Wall Chart*. Chicago: Claritian Publications, 1992.

   This attractive wall chart is organized around an historical timeline that runs from the 18th century to the 1990s. On one side of the timeline is a listing of major historical events. On the other side, a listing of Catholic social teaching documents including a brief summary of their content. (Note: The chart is no longer in print but it has been placed on the following web site: www.uscatholic.org/cstline/tline.html.)

COLLECTIONS OF OFFICIAL SOCIAL TEACHING DOCUMENTS

- David J. O'Brien and Thomas A. Shannon, ed., *Catholic Social Thought: The Documentary Heritage*. Maryknoll, NY: Orbis Books, 1995.

   This is a very comprehensive compendium of Catholic social encyclicals and other official papal documents on Catholic social teaching. It includes the U.S. bishops' pastoral letters on peace and on economic justice. It is indexed by subject and author and is available in paperback.
- Michael Walsh and Brian Davies, ed., *Proclaiming Justice and Peace: Papal Documents from Rerum Novarum through Centesimus Annus.* Mystic, CT: Twenty-Third Publications, 1991.

   This is another good compendium of official documents.
- Joseph Donders, ed., *John Paul II: The Encyclicals in Everyday Language*. Maryknoll, NY: Orbis Books, 1995.

   This is a compendium of Pope John Paul II's encyclicals presented in a translation that is much more easily read than the sometimes dense prose of the original texts. It is not an official translation but it very accurately reflects the content of the official texts.

COMMENTARIES

- Donal Dorr, *Option for the Poor: A Hundred Years of Vatican Social Teaching*. Maryknoll, NY: Orbis Books, 1992.

   This is an excellent commentary for those who want a more in-depth review of the Catholic social tradition. The author reviews the tradition thoroughly, examines historical developments in the teaching, and lifts up the moral theme of care for the poor.

- J. A. Coleman, SJ, ed., *One Hundred Years of Catholic Social Thought*. Maryknoll, NY: Orbis Books, 1991.

  This is an excellent collection of essays by a wide range of authors. The six general essays on Catholic social teaching are especially useful. The remainder of the book is divided into three sections that cover the themes of the family, work and economics, justice, and peace.

- Charles E. Curran and Richard A. Mc Cormick, SJ, eds., *Readings in Moral Theology: Official Catholic Social Teaching, No. 5*. New York: Paulist Press, 1986.

  This is an excellent collection of essays and commentaries on Catholic social thought. It includes a wide range of authors and a diverse body of content. In short, it is one of the best collections of commentaries on this topic.

- Charles E. Curran, *American Catholic Social Ethics: Twentieth Century Approaches*. Notre Dame, IN: University of Notre Dame Press, 1982.

  This work discusses Catholic social ethics in the American context by analyzing the contributions of key individuals who helped shape American Catholic social thought in this century. Distinct chapters are devoted to John A. Ryan, William Engelen (Central-Verein), Paul Hanly Furfey (Catholic Worker), John Courtney Murray, and James W. Douglass (Catholic Peace Movement).

- John Haughey, ed., *The Faith That Does Justice — Examining the Christian Source for Social Change*. New York: Paulist Press, 1977.

  A very useful collection of essays by scholars such as Avery Dulles, John Donahue, John Langan, Jr., David Hollenbach, and John Haughley. The essay by Donahue on biblical justice is a very good overview. The essay by Hollenbach entitled "Modern Catholic Social Teachings Concerning Justice" is an excellent summary.

- Michael and Kenneth Himes, *Fullness of Faith*. Mahwah, NJ: Paulist Press, 1993.

    This is a very insightful work that provides theological reflection on Catholic social thought and public theology. Notable chapters include "Original Sin," "The Trinity and Human Rights," "Grace and a Consistent Ethic of Life," and "The Communion of Saints and an Ethic of Solidarity." It is a very thoughtful and inspiring work.

- William L. Droel and Greg Pierce, *Confident and Competent — A Challenge for the Lay Church*. Notre Dame, IN: Ave Maria Press, 1987.

    This small paperback provides an insightful and straightforward challenge to lay persons to fulfill the Vatican Council's mandate "to be Church in the world". The authors contend that lay spirituality is based on "work in the world". This book contains excellent brief treatments of topics such as the definition of social justice, social teaching, and the spirituality of work.

- David Hollenbach, *Claims in Conflict — Retrieving and Renewing the Catholic Human Rights Tradition*. New York: Paulist Press, 1979.

    This is a clear and thoughtful work that summarizes and analyzes Catholic social teaching on the topic of human rights. It situates Catholic teaching in the context of the wider public debate about human rights, both nationally and internationally. This is a very useful work that helps interpret one of the foundational themes of the Church's social teachings.

- Daniel C. Maguire, *The Moral Core of Judaism and Christianity*. Minneapolis: Augsburg Fortress, 1993.

    This is a powerful and bold attempt to refute the myth that there is no commonality in the Jewish and Christian traditions of moral thought. The theme of justice is prominent in this work. It provides a good opportunity to better understand Catholic social teaching in the wider context of Judeo-Christian thought.

- Charles Avila, *Ownership — Early Christian Teaching.* Maryknoll, NY: Orbis Books, 1983.

     This is a rich anthology of early Church teachings on the theme of ownership. Patristic writers in the third and fourth centuries had a surprisingly radical and consistent tradition of thought on ownership and property. Works of St. Clement of Alexandria, St. Basil the Great, St. Ambrose, St. John Chrysostom, and St. Augustine are among those included.

INTERNET RESOURCES ON CATHOLIC SOCIAL TEACHING

http://www.osjspm.org/cst

This web site is a comprehensive source for Catholic social teaching documents and resources. It includes virtually all the official texts of the papal encyclicals on social justice as well as other social teaching documents. It also includes key quotations organized by specific themes, a list of resources for educators, and links to other related web sites.

http://www.osjspm.org/justed.htm

This is the justice education page of the Office for Social Justice in the Archdiocese of St. Paul and Minneapolis. It includes information on the Catholic Justice Educators' Network (CJEN), the archdiocesan network that supports and promotes the integration of social teaching in the schools and religious education programs of the archdiocese.

http://www.mcgill.pvt.k12.al.us/jerryd/cm/cst.htm

This web site lists over 100 links to official documents, commentaries, and other resources on Catholic social teaching.

http://salt.claretianpubs.org/

This web site, hosted by Claretian Publications, is a good all-around site for information and links on social justice.

http://www.seattlearch.org/reled/index.htm

This web site from the Archdiocese of Seattle describes a project in which educators are creating new resources on Catholic social teaching for Catholic schools and religious education programs. Lessons plans for different grade levels are posted on the site.

Appendix II

Major Documents of Modern Catholic Social Teaching

Vatican Documents

1891   *On the Condition of Labor   (Rerum Novarum)*   Pope Leo XIII

1931   *After Forty Years   (Quadragesimo Anno)*   Pope Pius XI

1961   *Mother and Teacher   (Mater et Magistra)*   Pope John XXIII

1963   *Peace on Earth   (Pacem in Terris)*   Pope John XXIII

1965   *Pastoral Constitution on the Church in the Modern World
        (Gaudium et Spes)*   Second Vatican Council

1967   *The Development of Peoples   (Populorum Progressio)*   Pope Paul VI

1971   *A Call to Action   (Octogesima Adveniens)*   Pope Paul VI

1971   *Justice in the World   (Justicia in Mundo)*   Synod of Bishops

1979   *Redeemer of Humanity   (Redemptor Hominis)*   Pope John Paul II

1981   *On Human Work   (Laborem Exercens)*   Pope John Paul II

1988   *On Social Concern   (Solicitudo Rei Socialis)*   Pope John Paul II

1991   *The One Hundredth Year   (Centesimus Annus)*   Pope John Paul II

1995   *The Gospel of Life   (Evangelium Vitae)*   Pope John Paul II

U.S. Bishops' Documents

1983   *The Challenge of Peace*

1986   *Economic Justice for All: Catholic Social Teaching and the U.S. Economy*

About the Author

Mr. Ronald Krietemeyer began his career at the National Conference of Catholic Bishops. From 1978-1987, he served as the chief staff person for the committee of bishops that drafted the 1986 pastoral letter on the economy. In this capacity, he assisted the bishops in the consultation, research, and drafting that were part of the five-year process leading up to the publication of the letter. He also served as the Director of the Office of Domestic Policy advising and assisting the bishops on domestic social policy issues at the national level. From 1987-1989, Mr. Krietemeyer taught social ethics at the College of St. Thomas in St. Paul, MN.

Currently, he is the Director of the Office for Social Justice in the Archdiocese of Saint Paul and Minneapolis. In this capacity, he coordinates and organizes advocacy and educational efforts that focus on economic and social justice for low-income constituencies. He also advises and trains Church leaders in the field of Catholic social teaching and social action. Additionally, he speaks widely on social teaching and social action and writes a bi-weekly column for the *Catholic Spirit* newspaper.

Mr. Krietemeyer has a bachelor's degree in Latin American Studies from Josephinum College in Columbus, OH, a master's degree in Theology from St. John's University in Collegeville, MN, and a master's degree in Public Affairs from Humphrey Institute University of Minnesota in Minneapolis, MN.